JOHN WILKES – THE AYLESBURY YEARS (1747-176...

To some John Wilkes was a Friend to Liberty; a champion endeavouring to uphold the freed... government censorship saw that its activities were kept secret to but a few, and when, in particular, Commons were suppressed. The cry Wilkes and Liberty was echoed loudly by the mob when, f... election as a Member of Parliament for Middlesex was declared void by a vote in the House; this m... years after he had severed all connections with Aylesbury. So who was John Wilkes – rebel, rake and roué – or a popular patriot - and what was his earlier connection with the small market town of Aylesbury?

Wilkes was born in Clerkenwell around 1725, the second son of a self-made malt distiller. As one of the many rising middle class families of the mid 18th century, his mother, Sarah (Heaton), a Presbyterian by conviction and inclination was determined that her son, although not born a gentleman, should be educated as one; at no time was it suggested that he should join his father in the family business. After five years at a private school in Hertford, John was sent to the Reverend Matthew Leeson's school in Thame. Within a few years the school was moved to Aylesbury under the patronage of Mrs Mary Mead, the widow of a wealthy London merchant whose brother-in-law, William had built Prebendal House in the town in the early part of the century; hence the first link was forged with Aylesbury, albeit a tenuous one.

Leyden University in the Netherlands, which was founded by William of Orange in 1575, was chosen as the next stage in Wilkes' education that, accompanied by Leeson, he entered in 1744. This was followed by further travels throughout the protestant Rhineland – not the Grand Tour undertaken at that time by the sons of wealthy landowning families but sufficient to stimulate a young mind on matters which concerned him. Upon his return to England, however, plans were afoot for an arranged marriage between John and Mary Mead, the daughter of Leeson's Aylesbury patron., Mrs Mary Mead.

She was related to William Mead, a wealthy linen draper and dyer from London, who came to live in Aylesbury until his death in 1724, and built Prebendal House in Aylesbury in the early 18th century. In retirement he continued to be active in the affairs of the town as High Sheriff in 1716 and, as joint executor with his brother of the estate of Henry Phillips of London, he was responsible and instrumental in the building of the new Grammar School in Aylesbury that is now incorporated within the County Museum. He was buried at Soulbury where there were family connections.

Together with his younger brother John, he was apprenticed to London Livery Companies; each is shown in the '*1695 Return of London Inhabitants Within The Walls*' as successful merchants. John, a London citizen and grocer, died in 1717 leaving his widow and daughter, both named Mary, a considerable fortune as well as making generous bequests to the Overseers and "The Poor of Great Brickhill, the place of my nativity".

Upon his death in 1724, brother William, who does not appear to have married, willed the lease of the Parsonage of Aylesbury to his unmarried sisters Rebeckia (Rebecca) and Mary and thereafter to Mary Mead, the daughter of his late brother John. Mary predeceased her sister, Rebecca by three years and in her will, she (Rebecca) confirmed the terms of the lease in favour of her niece Mary who at 17 was still a minor and consequently very much under her mother's supervision; Mrs Mead remained a dominant influence throughout the whole of Mary's Wilkes' life.

The marriage of John Wilkes and Miss Mary Mead took place on 23 May 1747 at St John's, Clerkenwell, close to the family home of both the Wilkes at St James' Square and the Mead family in Red Lion Square; the bride was 30, nine years older than the groom. She was baptised on 9 October 1716 at St Sepulchre's, a parish south of Clerkenwell; the marriage settlement was generous. In addition to the lease of the Prebendal estate in Aylesbury, there were many properties in north Bucks and adjoining Bedfordshire attached to it.

Within five years the couple had drifted apart, each going their own way after the birth of their only child, Polly in 1750, three years after the marriage; he aspired to the high life in London which contrasted to the God fearing family in Red Lyon Square. In 1752 the trustees amended the marriage agreement and allowed ownership of the Prebendal lease to pass into Wilkes's sole hands ensuring his finance independence from the Mead and Sherbrook families who had hitherto held the purse strings. Four years later a legal separation was agreed to that gave him custody of his daughter Polly and the considerable marriage settlement estates in exchange for an annuity to his wife of £200 per annum. In later life he was reported as saying that "I hated my wife but was the civilest husband to her."

Now free of the restraints of his wife's family, Wilkes entered into his role of lord of the Manor with gusto with the improvement of his Aylesbury property. He became involved in local affairs in an increasing manner, High Sheriff for the county, a Justice of the Peace, a captain in the Militia and a trustee of the Free Grammar School and of Bedford's Charity to mention but few. His involvement in the establishment of a branch of the London Foundling Hospital in the town was one of his less savoury achievements due to financial mismanagement and indeed possible misappropriation of funds entrusted to him. He also set about expanding the estate by adjacent property purchases and in particular his garden of which he was inordinately proud. The letters between him and his political agent, John Dell, which form the bulk of this paper, give an insight into Dell's involvement in many of these activities but it must be emphasised that Wilkes' future achievements and failures in the national scheme of things do not form part of this record but are worth mentioning in brief.

During the second term as one of the Members for Aylesbury, Wilkes, with others in London, launched the now famous, or some would say infamous, weekly political publication *The North Briton* that satirised the government of the day; it could be likened to a *Private Eye* of 1762. Things were brought to a head when in No.**45,** the King's Tory minister Lord Bute was lampooned over his connections with his Royal Master's household. It also attacked the King's speech from the throne at the opening of Parliament – an unheard of event; it provoked King George to call his tormenter, "That Devil, Wilkes."

Warrants were issued for the arrest of Wilkes for the so-called libel and his house was ransacked; his papers, both private and political, were seized. Now committed as a close prisoner to the Tower, there began a long drawn out legal battle resulting in Wilkes' imprisonment in the Kings' Bench Prison; outlawry followed and his Aylesbury estate was sold after his release and flight abroad. After a few years however he returned to this country a national hero culminating in his election as Lord Mayor of London in 1774.

The bulk of the so called Wilkes/Dell letters were written between 1753 and 1762 by John Wilkes to his friend and political agent, John Dell, an Aylesbury farmer, brewer and general factotum. Like Wilkes, Dell had a Presbyterian upbringing and they may well have known each other at Dr Leeson's seminary at Thame which, as has been seen, came to Aylesbury in 1747 under the patronage of Mrs Mary Mead, the widow of John Mead(e) d.1716, a wealthy London merchant. Dell was two years older than Wilkes and, as an entry in the Aylesbury register reveals, the baptism - John son of Jacob and Lydia Dell - was performed by Mr Ward.

John Dell was born on 24 July 1723 and baptised seven days later at St Mary's Aylesbury by Mr Ward, the Presbyterian Minister. He was the youngest child and only surviving son of Jacob Dell, a maltster of the town. Jacob Dell senior, another maltster living in Aylesbury, appears in the Poll Book of 1705 for the county. In his will, which was proved in 1727, he stated that he was living with his kinsman Jacob, the son of Jeremiah who in turn was said to be the son of John Dell and Rebecca Gaskin/Gascoigne. This couple were married in High Wycombe in 1640; he was of Aylesbury and was buried there in 1676. In the Clergy Returns for 1669 he was entered as allowing his house to be used for worship by people described as "most Presbyterians". The family's Presbyterian connection continued for many years but like Wilkes himself, the Anglican Church was an easier place with which to be associated in Georgian England.

John Dell was a man of many parts and has been described as a farmer and brewer as well as a Surveyor of the Highways of Aylesbury. As a trustee of the Bedford's Charity, the body governing these highway matters which at one time included Wilkes himself; this was not a parochial appointment there being others acting for the parish. He was one of the growing-class of 18th century men without direct political influence but with sufficient local knowledge to be worth cultivating by those in power. It is doubtful that he ever voted in a county election where the franchise was restricted to freeholders having tenements to the annual value of 40 shillings but, however, it was a different matter in borough elections where there was a wide variance in the electoral qualification.

There was no electoral roll as such and at every election those wishing to vote turned up to establish their entitlement so to do. One of these in Aylesbury and other places, together with "scot and lot", was that of a potwalloper which was defined as a person who, although in shared accommodation, possessed a hearth on which to boil his own pot provided he had not been in receipt of poor relief for a year and thus enjoyed some economic independence. With his local knowledge, Dell was to prove a valuable ally in the battle for votes in Aylesbury.

For those aspiring to political power in the days before universal suffrage, local contacts were essential as the member was seldom resident or even local and once elected was seldom seen again but needed to be kept abreast of any thing or any body which might threaten future prospects of power.

There is evidence that Dell was previously acting for Thomas Potter, the member for Aylesbury until the latter's resignation in 1757, and it is interesting to note that members of the Dell family continued to act for candidates in subsequent elections well into the 19th century. John Dell's son, Thomas (1760-1821) and grandsons Thomas (1791-1833) and John (1793-1852) acted for William Rickford, the founder of the Aylesbury Old Bank and member for the borough for 23 years,

One thing which the correspondence reveals (the letters are one way as there are none from Dell to Wilkes; perhaps they were destroyed when Wilkes London house was raided by the authorities in 1762), is the latter's undoubted strong sense of humour – a literal leg pulling if you will; but Wilkes knows what he wants of his agent particularly in domestic matters and the management of his Prebendal estate in Aylesbury; where Leeson's school had been housed. Wilkes already displays the guile and charm that in later years served him well in his dealings with less provincial matters.

The letters give an insight into local events evolving here in Aylesbury. Mixed with the mundane, however, are local as well as national events in the short nine years or so covered by the correspondence. For example we know now that Dell and his family were guests of Wilkes at the coronation of King George The Third in 1761, not seated in the Abbey but perched in one of the stands overlooking the scene. It follows therefore that Wilkes' conflict with the King and his ministry, for which he was later to be famous, was in the future and perhaps this is one reason why the correspondence has been largely ignored by earlier scholars of Wilkes' life; the existence of them was thought not to have been known to such biographers as Bleackley and Almon.

The letters, 78 in all, written by John Wilkes to his parliamentary agent John Dell, came down through the Dell family to his descendants, one of whom was Dr Thomas G Parrott (1860-1951), a stalwart of the Buckinghamshire Archaeological Society, who presented transcripts of the letters to the Society in 1920. They are held under reference 1920.107.1-78. The Buckinghamshire Local Studies have the self same copies under - DX 463.

The originals are now in the William L Clements Library, University of Michigan in the United States of America and form part of the larger Wilkes Collection. A single letter would appear to have been detached from the others, possibly whilst being transcribed prior to the sale to Mr Clements. This is dated 6 January 1761 and is now in the Society's collection.

The letters have been sorted chronologically irrespective of their content. Where only the day and month without the year are given, reference has been made to a perpetual calendar or in other cases from the national events contained in them; in a few cases assumptions have been made and consequently may be out of sequence.

2

It must be emphasized that, as the title suggests, the letters and the comments to them, cover the Aylesbury years in Wilkes' earlier career and no attempt has been made to delve deeper into what was a complex and far-reaching period in Georgian England.

Many others, highly qualified in the literary world, have been along that path but it is hoped that the letters will form part of a greater insight into Wilkes' connections with Aylesbury that has hitherto been largely ignored by others. To those with Aylesbury interests, many of the names in them will be familiar although the exact context or significance is not immediately obvious. Clearly Wilkes' circle of acquaintances on the national scene was considerable but reference to them in the letters is often mixed with the mundane. Dell, referred to in one letter as "Old Faithful", was clearly used as a sounding board as to local opinion but in many other ways a whipping boy when things appeared to be spinning out of control.

OTHER LETTERS BY WILKES

The letters reproduced here are published in full for the first time. There is no modern collection of Wilkes letters to match those published for Burke or Disraeli. However, many of Wilkes other letters were published in the eighteenth and early nineteenth century. Most of these publications are now to be found on the internet as e-books. For instance, the Internet Archive (http://www.archive.org/index).

a. Letters, from the year 1774 to the year 1796, addresses to his daughter, the late Miss Wilkes : with a collection of his miscellaneous poems, to which is prefixed a memoir of the life of Mr. Wilkes (Volume 1-3)
b. The speeches of Mr. Wilkes in the House of commons
c. The correspondence of the late John Wilkes, with his friends, printed from the original manuscripts, in which are introduced memoirs of his life (Volume 2-5) - Wilkes, John, 1727-1797
d. The North Briton, from no. I to no. XLVI. inclusive : with several useful and explanatory notes, not printed in any former edition : to which is added, a copious index to every name and article

COVER Portrait is a copy of a painting by T Hudson, circa 1774 (Buckinghamshire County Museum)

John Wilkes, Statue, Fetter Lane. London

Aylesbury
Oct. 26. 1760.

Sir,

The great and important event of yesterday makes it necessary for me to lose no time in renewing my applications to this Borough. I take the liberty of entreating the honour of your support and protection, which I shall ever most gratefully acknowledge.

I am, with much respect,

Sir, your very humble
Servant,

John Wilkes.

Sir William Lee Bar.t

Copy of my Answer Oct.r 31.st 1760

Sir I have this Day the favour of y.r dated 26.th ca w.t you do me the Hon.r to ask an Interest w.h I am very sensible is scarce worth yr acceptance and I wish I cou'd give you an explicit answer upon the subject but I have some engagements at this time w.h I doubt not y self wou'd think a reasonable excuse & therefore hope you will not less esteem me
Sir &c.

A letter from Wilkes seeking Sir William Lees' vote and a copy of the latter's reply
(Buckinghamshire Archaeological Society Collection)

Great George Street
Jan. 6. 1761.

Surviving Wilkes/Dell Letter in England (Buckinghamshire Archaeological Society Collection)

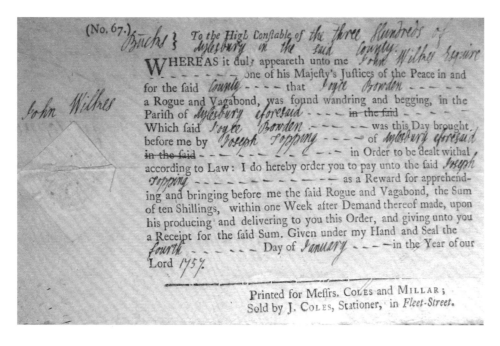

Certificate of Registration as a Magistrate 1757 (Buckinghamshire Archaeological Society Collection)

W/19 – Dec.11 1751 London

Dear Sir

The weather is so severe, and there is even here so dreary a snow prospect, that I am afraid I shall not for some days be able to muster up resolution enough to quit this charming warm, wicked town - In the meantime I am inform'd that you have had a visit from Aylesbury from the two brothers, the Willes's. -I am impatient to know if you all comforted them under the rigour of the season, or whether you gave them a reception as cold as that - You will oblige me, if you will give me a particular account by the return of post - Has your Father finish'd the list he was to make out of all the voting houses, distinguishing them according to the streets? I can only tell you by letter that the Willes's went without saying one word to Mr Potter or me, and against a half promise to have din'd at Mr Potter's last Sunday – Mr Potter will soon come and talk to our good people in the proper way – I desire my service to Mrs Dell, Miss Sukey, your Father, Mr Stephens etc. and am,

Your most humble servant   John Wilkes

I have just now your letter for which I thank you. Pray let me hear all particulars by the return of the post.

This is the first letter in the series to his agent John Dell and sets the scene for the future relationship with him, which was to become more intimate in the next few years. Wilkes was hopeful of putting-up as joint candidate with Thomas Potter, the second son of John Potter, the Bishop of Oxford and later Archbishop of Canterbury, but he was frustrated in this when Potter allied himself with Willes.

The brothers John and Edward Willes were the sons of Sir John Willes, a lawyer who became chief justice of common pleas. Edward sat as Aylesbury's member of Parliament between 1747-1754 and in this letter Wilkes was clearly sounding out his agent as to the townsfolk's reaction to the visit and in particular of the possibility of John Willes putting up for election if Edward had decided not to stand again.
As a pacifier Wilkes was appointed to the office of High Sheriff for the county and with it went the power to appoint the returning officer. see W/4

The newly appointed Prime Minister, the Duke of Newcastle, suggested that Wilkes should fight, at his own expense, the Delval family seat of Berwick-upon-Tweed. Although confident of success, he failed in this.

Miss Sukey (Susannah) was Dell's sister (d.1768) who was later to become the wife of Revd. John Stephens, vicar of Aylesbury and he, a drinking partner of Wilkes. Dell's father was Jacob Dell, a maltster of Aylesbury, who died in October, the following year.

W/4 – Tuesday morning. January 15 (1754)

Dear Sir

I have only a minute's time, while Parker is waiting, to tell you that I have consented to the persuasion of two or three particular friends, for some important services, and that I am to serve this year as High Sheriff. Be as silent as the grave, only whisper Stephens when you see him that he is to be my chaplain if he pleases. Price will be Under Sheriff, and has been with me in town to promise absolute obedience. I am going to the Duke of Marlborough – you see I declare myself throughout a friend to liberty, and will act up to it - Write to me in a post or two.

Your friend and humble servant
John Wilkes

This letter has no year but it was clearly 1754, the year of Wilkes' appointment as High Sheriff. John Stephens, the vicar of Aylesbury, was later to become Dell's brother-in-law when he married his (Dell's) sister, Susannah at Aylesbury in 1761. Wilkes signed the register as a witness.

Wilkes declares himself at this early stage in his political career to be a "Friend To Liberty". He repeated this phrase a great deal in later years.

Price was Edward Price, a local solicitor and Trustee of Hardings, a local charity of some repute. Custom had it that a solicitor always held the position of Under Sheriff. This custom has continued to this day.

W/20 – April 2 1754 London

Dear Sir

I have just wrote a publick letter to you, to be communicated to whoever you think proper, lest, in case of an opposition; from my not being at the election, I might be thought cool towards Mr Potter, or to have drop'd him. Nothing but an election of my own (entre nous) cou'd have kept me from you. But if I apprehended danger to Mr Potter, I wou'd give up my own election to secure him. I think him particularly happy in having so clever and fit an agent as yourself. My warmest wishes attend you. Pray take care he is nam'd first in the return. It is a point of honour. I beg you to write to me regularly; direct as usual, and your letters will be sent to me. I am at a certainty of a trifling expense if I do not succeed. Do not omit writing Thursday night. My particular compliments to your Father, Mr Stephens etc. and believe me ever, Dear Sir

Your most humble Servant John Wilkes
Whatever you think I shou'd, tho I am not present at the election, I wou'd willingly do. Let me know freely your sentiments. My not coming to the election shou'd be at present a secret. As to meeting Willes etc. etc., I wish my friends to consult Mr Potter and follow his opinion. I hope Mr Potter in everything will take the lead. Adieu, dear Jack. God bless you.

Tuesday night eleven. Charge all letters to me

This, and the two previous letters, shows that this is early on in the Wilkes/Dell relationship. Wilkes indicates here his continuing support for Potter in his effort to be elected and makes it clear that he expects full support from his Aylesbury friends in helping Potter to this end although he himself will not participate in person.

W/3 - Sat noon (1754)

Dear Dell

I am very willing to have the day for the delivery of the lists put off, and I wish you to get Paten to send directions according to the several Parishes. I wish it however deferr'd only till the Wednesday following, as we shall then all of us be in the country. I am here ready to set out, whenever I receive your commands, good Mr Returning Officer. If you do not send any, I shall be with you on Tuesday to dinner, which I beg you to order for me, and good fires.

Ever yours John Wilkes

Marlow Saturday noon.

Mr Burt is canvassing here with great spirit and success so, that I fear poor Moore falls.

Robert Paten was one of Aylesbury's Churchwardens. The lists to which Wilkes refers are those he asked Dell's father to compile six months ago from his knowledge of the Aylesbury electorate. These have been delayed   probably due to illness. (Jacob, the father, died in October 1754).

Daniel Moore was elected Member for Great Marlow in 1754 with William Churchill so Wilkes' forebodings were not justified. Wilkes' post-script dates this letter.

Derby Porcelain figurine of Wilkes (Buckinghamshire County Museum)

W/21 – Oct 16 1754 Berwick

Dear Dell

I am much oblig'd by your letter which is the most extraordinary I ever read: for I never before knew a farmer talk of being easy and contented. I hope you will always have as good times, and I do not doubt you will find as good a disposition to enjoy them. We are all as highly pleas'd here as you can be with a fine harvest: and we have a new crop of votes ready, whenever we will. I am so hurr'd with agreeable (sic) business (tho' Sunday) I have not time, nor is it safe in a letter, to say more but I must add as I know it will givyou pleasure, that the prospect before me is very clear and engaging, and not distant. Every thing will answer beyond my expectation. I go from hence on Wednesday, and only stay two days at my old friend Lord Gallway', in my way to London. You may freely use the old bricks you desire. I will not believe one syllable you say about the Jail. I wou'd still go on with our game chaps. I am pleas'd you like my garden. I beg my service to your Father, Mrs Dell, Miss Sukey etc and am, Dear Dell, your oblig'd humble servant

John Wilkes

I shall be in Aylesbury, soon after I am in London

Wilkes' anticipation of a "fine harvest with a crop of votes ready" was not borne out for he failed to take the Berwick seat despite the money he had to hand out. His optimism is still apparent in W/23 but when it came to the vote he received only 192 to the 307 of John Delval whose family had clashed with Prime Minister Pelham. A local man Thomas Watson topped the poll with 374 votes. See W/19.

W/22 Nov 28 1754 London

Dear Dell

I have now entirely to my satisfaction got my Parliamentary business into the House and you will see by the votes, an early day appointed us as well as a hearing at the Bar. I hope now to get into the country for three or four days at least, and intend to be in Aylesbury Saturday afternoon. I beg the favour of you to order Margaret to get for our supper a neck of mutton and broth, and two roast fowls and to lay in a sur-loin of beef, a leg of pork, a fillet of veal, two fowls and a pair of rabbits, in order to chase hunger from our doors: not forgetting good fires in the dining room and best parlour, to chase away the cold, which at present in London is very extreme. Smart's son call'd upon me here, and ask'd for his Father's place; but I told him I was engag'd. I wish you wou'd order in directly five gallons of ale, and as much small beer from Barretts'. I make loud complaints of you as a gamekeeper, but more of this when we meet. My compliments to all friends. I am your most humble servant

John Wilkes

This is but one of the letters given over to domestic matters and clearly Wilkes was not willing to starve on his pending few day's visit to Aylesbury.

The Prebendal with the garden front shortly before restoration,
photo *Hills Harris (Oxford) Ltd from Hugh Hanleys's book on the building.*

Dear Dell

I receiv'd your letter yesterday and congratulations on the <u>important</u> honour conferr'd on me by the Feoffees. I am surpris'd at their other choice, because I always understood that no person cou'd be chose into that trust, who was not a house-keeper at Aylesbury. As to Sir W being their tenant, I do not think there is much in that: I am rather pleas'd with it, because it may soon be our case without any murmuring, now the example is set. I suspect you have been too secure, perhaps lazy; but we will take effectual measures against the next vacancy. At present you have lost no honour, considering the <u>immense dignity</u> of the <u>two worthy</u> gentlemen, who are chose: therefore be comforted – and comfort your wife in this cold weather. I am glad to hear my garden is emerging from that state of chaos it has long been in; I hope Stephens will restore it to beauty & order. Pray tell him how kindly I take his bestowing so much pains on it. I long to hear that the plantations are finish'd. I wish he wou'd send to Lowndes about the Elms; as I cannot yet come into the country. Either Lowndes or his gardener wou'd fully direct any body about the taking them up. The best spread trees shou'd be planted before the front of the Dove-house but to be strip up about seven foot.

I am much surpris'd at what you mention of the quantity of game lately sent me; for I have neither feather nor lever these three weeks. I except a single partridge sent me by Terry. Pray explain this mystery, or is it a fraud of the waggoners, or my own servants? I can never have too much game.

As to Berwick, we are very easy and safe; but this cursed Oxfordshire business tires out everybody, and must be gone thro – and will I suppose before new year's day. I know not if I shou'd lessen myself so much as to tell it to an Aylesbury man, but every soul here cries me up to the skies as an <u>uncorrupt</u> Patriot. Fie on Mr P and Mr W. Has Willes sent any wheat? Are you not very dry after Mr Potter's? We concerted that scheme together. Price will give you directions about the constableship. There is no such book as you mention of Fieldings. There is of Sanders Welch's but it is wrote for the London officers and wou'd be of no use to you in the country. Poor Mr Leeson! I paid him the tribute of a few tears from the recollection of past scenes tho' I take it his death was a great deliverance to himself, as well as every one about him. He had formerly left me in his will a few old medals; but I suppose of late had dispos'd otherways of them: I wish however you wou'd enquire of them, and what became of his books, but not in my name.

I hope soon to be in Aylesbury; but really how soon I cannot say. I want my planting finished as soon as possible; but my greatest want of all is Chilton, the Butcher's land; which I covert most inordinately, not withstanding the tenth commandment. Can you no way contrive to get it for me? If you cannot, I must come and set you all a blaze there again. My compliments to all my friends, Mrs Dell, Miss Sukey and Mr Stephens in particular.
I am, Dear Dell, your friend and humble servant. John Wilkes

I spent my Christmas with Mr Potter in Bedfordshire, but the roads to Leighton, and from hence to Aylesbury were so bad I could not come over to you.

Wilkes was elected by the Feoffees (Trustees) of the Bedford Charity around this date but he is clearly less impressed by their other choice of Sir W (Lee) of Hartwell. Nevertheless Lee's appointment indicates to Wilkes that a precedent had been made and he hints to Dell about the next appointment. Dell was, in fact, appointed in July 1755 when a vacancy occurred. The Bedford Charity was established under the will of John Bedford in the 15th century, as amended in 1597, and related to lands given to the perpetual repair and amendment of the Highways of Aylesbury.

In the coded messages in this letter, Wilkes is anxious to know how much Willes and Potter have come up with in bribes or if there have been conversations with the electorate when he asks about wheat and how dry they are. See also W/21 concerning the Berwick contest.

Dell's appointment as Constable has caused him to seek advice from Wilkes as to his duties in that position and asks if there is a book to guide him as to procedures. Saunders Welch (1711-1784) was High Constable of Holborn and an appointed assistant to John Fielding – The Blind Beak. In the previous year (1754) Welch had published a volume entitled "Observations on the Office of Constable with cautions for the more safe execution of that duty". Wilkes was of the opinion, however, that as it was written for the London officers, it would be of little assistance to Dell in his new position.

(Edward) Price was a local solicitor with whom Wilkes dealt. His (Wilkes') plans for adding to his properties in the town are also apparent in this letter. In particular he is anxious to acquire the land of William Chilton, a butcher in the town. The piece of land was no doubt used as grazing for Chilton's cattle and must have abutted Wilkes' estate although it has not been positively identified as such.

Dr Mathew Leeson, the Headmaster of the Thame School that Wilkes attended, died early in 1755. His will describes him "of New Thame, Oxfordshire."

W/24– Feb.27. 1755 London

Dear Dell

I send this by Peter, who goes on private business to Mr Edwards. I was very much pleas'd with your letter. I wou'd give Chilton £100 (tho' it is a most extravagant price) for the ground, and he shou'd have every individual thing on the premises, but then he shou'd be oblig'd to remove them in three months. As to Read's house, I wou'd do him all the service I cou'd, but would article nothing about it. If I bought the house etc. at the price of the bricks etc. I should have little objection, but I prefer only buying the land. If you can fix Chilton, do, and let Price proceed with the writings as fast as possible, for fear of accidents, or change of mind. Be as secret as the case admits, and do no lose one minute.

I shall certainly come to Aylesbury Saturday the 8th March, but Mr P is uncertain. There is some truth in the story you mention of Mr E.W. but I will tell you more when I see you. If you do not hear from me again, I wish you wou'd order me in a fillet of veal, a sirloin of beef, four fowls, and a couple of rabbits besides all sorts of game, for I do not chose to be starved among you. Manage Chilton's affair cheap and well and I will advance you a year's salary as gamekeeper, tho' you behave very ill in that post. Mrs Wilkes and I desire our compliments to Mrs Dell, Miss Sukey, Mr Stephens etc.

I am, Dear Dell, your friend and humble servant. John Wilkes

Good fires for Saturday Seven nights; and neck of mutton and broth and beef stakes (sic) for supper. Hope to see my garden most prodigiously neat. Pray tell Mr Stephens so. On second thoughts I send this by the post

This is anticipating one of Wilkes visits to his Aylesbury property to which he trying to augment; clearly he does not choose to be starved whilst out of London. Edward Price, a fellow trustee of the Harding Charity, was one of Aylesbury's solicitors acting for Wilkes on various occasions. Wilkes has offered £100 for "Chilton's land" although the figure is thought to be extravagant.

Wilkes again returns to the question of game about which he is clearly enthusiastic. He calls Dell his gamekeeper but perhaps it was a question of the cost and the local supply rather than what he saw as inflated London prices.

Dell has obviously got wind that Edward Willes (EW) is thinking of standing down at the next election. See W/19.

W/25 – Sept.29.1755. Eleven o'clock Red Lion Court

Dear Dell

I am just return'd here and have got your letter, which I am very well pleas'd with. Go on boldly against Reading, and I will indemnify you, or rather the other offenders shall. It has you know the air of impartiality in the strongest degree, and tell Reading and every body, that had they applied to me, I myself would have convict'd you. I know Hill's skit, but it will not do. It is still a chance if Reading can get any body to prove the fact against you, but in all events I promise you shall be no sufferer, and Reading is a scoundrel. I wou'd punish at all events. Let me desire you to persuade Woodcock to go directly to Revett's to make affidavit, and do not regard what our timorous folks may tell you. It is of more importance than you at present imagine to carry it throughout, and if any person at Aylesbury is afterwards convicted, every mouth must be stop'd, when it is known I convicted you, or indeed let it go on.

I shall be in Aylesbury on Wednesday morning and wish you would sup with me but take no notice of this and get Woodcock to go to Revetts to make affidavit early on
Wednesday morning.

I am Dear Dell, your sincere friend, and humble servant, John Wilkes

Clearly Dell has over stepped the mark in some way in is dealing with the Aylesbury poor folk and is concerned about possible repercussions. Reading is well known to Wilkes as the accounts of the Overseers of the Poor for the town reveal and which, as a Justice of the Peace, he sanctioned. In the accounts for 18 November 1759 we read
"gave old Reading 6s. to buy some linen and go away." The "old scoundrel" Reading was clearly a thorn in the side of the Aylesbury authorities and Wilkes seems to be in favour of cutting him down to size.

W/26 – Nov. 22. 1755

Dear Dell

I intended the next week to have paid you a visit in Buckinghamshire, but I find so much business crowding upon me, that it will be impossible, and as I shall spend my Christmas among you, I shall hardly see Aylesbury till (sic) the 20th of December, when I return there from our turnpike meeting that day at Agmondesham. I shall be oblig'd to you to direct brewing for two hogsheads of keeping beer to be bottled off next October, and let some of the small beer you take off from thence be put into small casks to serve me at Christmas. I do not know what sort of a brewer Thorpe is, and I had rather he was not spar'd from the garden: but use your own discretion in this, and let it be done as soon as you can. I am told there are many expensive customs at Aylesbury at Christmas time, particularly about St Thomas's Day. I wish you would let me know what they are, and what is expected from me. Perhaps I may constantly spend one Christmas at Aylesbury, and I wou'd now settle all those things as precedents. I shall stay in the country three weeks. I expect Bigg's affair to be finished every day, and will write to him by the post or coach when I have intelligence of it. We are all very well and in high spirits. Our friends (entre nous) will all fall, to rise higher I expect. Tho' I talk big still, yet Berwick is damn'd but from some things, I cannot write, I am better pleased than ever.

Pray, my dear Dell, write me all the nonsensical news of A. It diverts me here amid the graver things. P has absolutely abandon'd it. I am interrupted. must therefore conclude.

Your sincere friend and humble servant   John Wilkes

I write next post to Mr Stephens about my garden.
My compliments to Mrs Dell etc.etc.

There are several hints in this letter as to future tactics and what may be expected of him at Christmas in the way of "expensive customs". He is also becoming resigned that he will not succeed at Berwick in spite of earlier optimism shown in W/23.

This is probable a reference to William Bigg of Walton whose property dealings possibly over his barn were causing concern to the authorities.

W/27 – Nov. 27. 1755 London

Dear Dell

All our Buckinghamshire friends are out, with Mr Legge, Chancellor of the Exchequer and many others. Fox and Newcastle are join'd against our friends, tho' at variance with each other in many important things. The chief of which is the disposition of places. In this strange confusion, the Chief Justice bids fair to get Jack Willes in some paltry place or other. I am detirmin'd to oppose him, and will attack him with the utmost spirit in every way, particularly the true Aylesbury way of palmistry. Be assured I will at any expense carry my point. It is of importance to the situation of my friends, as well as my own. The Packingtons are with us; but above all St Thomas Guinea. Potter has just left me, and will be down with you to canvass for me. It is only for this time, but I must and will carry it.   I am ready at half an hour's warning, and do not fail to let me have the first advices possible of anything done. Whatever you promise I will make good. The moment any thing is begun, declare me a candidate, and say I am on the road. I wish you wou'd make me out a list of all the streets in Aylesbury, and then mark the houses in each street that vote, and their present possessions, and take care nobody intrudes into the Parish. Every thing is at present a secret between you and Mr Stephens, and I beg it may continue so, unless any things happen for, possibly it may not before Christmas. Let me beg you to be on your guard against any alarm, and regard no expense of expresses by Woodcock etc.

I am, in great haste.

Your sincere friend John Wilkes.

Biggs' affair is about finished.

The Chancellor of the Exchequer, the Hon. Henry Bilson-Legge succeeded Sir William Lee of Hartwell who died in office in April 1754. but Legge lost office when he fell out of favour the following year along with many others of Wilkes' inclination and the administration appears in turmoil. Legge was Chancellor for short periods again in 1756 and 1757.

Wilkes was fond of his nicknames about all and sundry and St Thomas Guinea Potter was an obvious reference to his friend Thomas Potter who has been called Wilkes' mentor and "evil genius", the architect of the latter's excesses in Potter's lifetime. It is a clear reference to his open handedness to would-be supporters. Wilkes is ready to offer himself to the Aylesbury electorate but is waiting for the right moment before declaring his candidature. Dell is being asked to provide a list of voters and their status and to look out for "intruders" into the parish; only Dell and future brother-in-law, the Revd John Stephens (Stevens) are to know of Wilkes' plans, Who is Woodcock said to be worrying about the financial state of affairs? Could he be a man of this name who some years later was a partner in the banking firm of the Vale of Aylesbury Bank.

Dear Dell

I am greatly obliged to you for your letter, and the List, which must have given you no small trouble. I communicated it to Potter, who objects only to the small number of those who have rec'd alms, or have their rents paid, set at only four: but when you look into the Overseer's books, you will find them nearer forty, we imagine. At present it is not perhaps so near as we imagn'd; we are in the dark, but are sure of the earliest intelligence, which you shall have. Depend upon it, I will sink Willes by the weight of metal; and we shall be thought heroes, to turn a man out; the moment he has kiss'd hands for a place, that is to be a tool for Fox, or Newcastle. Potter thinks it absurd to declare, till I see whether Jack Willes gets anything or not; for he says I shall immediately feel all the bad consequences of an election, without a choice perhaps. I think he is right in this. I will however be ready, whenever you send for me, at any hour of the day or night. I approve of your scheme of a shilling for a widow, and half a crown for a poor family. What do you guess it will amount to?
I am sorry Bigg's affair is not finish'd but tell him I will not stop till I have serv'd him, and I am in daily expectation of the news. I receiv'd the birds safe. I agree with you, that it would be infinitely better for me to be chose for any other place: but where is that place now? I only mean Aylesbury <u>for this time</u>, and should laugh, when the rabble had got my money, to have the wretches come to ask favours of me. I will carry it with a high hand at the time, and higher still afterwards; and I will not a moment relax the wholesome discipline I have establish'd, be the consequences what they will. Charles Lowndes is my warm and steady friend. I will see every person you mention as soon as anything is certain.

I am sorry the Gentlemen Feoffes must be disappointed this time. I take the meeting to be an <u>ordinary</u> one; but in case of a vacancy in that or any other trust, I wou'd take post to Aylesbury, tho' I staid (sic) there but three hours, for I have all the trusts at heart. I think the Fable of the Fox & Goose is reviv'd ; but tho' the Fox has often carried off the goose, I never heard of the goose taking the Fox on his back, as Newcastle has done. I do not know whether our Buckinghamshire friends play a <u>safe</u> game, but they play a <u>great</u> game. I find you are quite a Newmarket. Sure the Carriers must get some money, notwithstanding all their complaints, to afford £50 betts (sic)

I am, with compliments to all our friends,

Dear Dell, your sincere friend & humble servant   John Wilkes

I hope the cod will be good, at least as good as Dudley's oysters, to an Aylesbury palate. I hope for a line in two or three days.

As requested in the previous letter, Dell has provided the details asked for including his estimate of those who have been in receipt of parish relief in the last year which, under the local electoral rules pertaining at this date, would invalidate their right to vote but clearly it is at variance with Wilkes and Potter who suggest that the figure is nearer 40 and the Overseers Books will, they say, show it to be so. John (Jack) Willes is still in possible contention as a candidate and Wilkes is clearly boasting of being thought a hero "to turn a man out who has kissed hands for a place".

Dell has clearly suggested who should be given "sweeteners" but as those he mentions would not possess a vote (a shilling for a widow and half a crown to a poor family) this would be but a gesture of good will. Dell has obviously also hinted that Wilkes should consider looking elsewhere to stand for election. Wilkes agrees but asks "where is that place?" and that he only wants Aylesbury "this time."

This is clearly a summons to a meeting of the Bedford Charity which Wilkes declines to attend but if a vacancy comes up in this or any other charity, he will make every effort to make his voice heard as he has all the Trusts at heart.

The reference to the fable of the Fox and Goose is a comment on the political situation of 1755 and the unholy alliance between Thomas Pellam-Holles, 1st Duke of Newcastle (1693-1768), 1st Lord of the Treasury and Henry Fox, 1st Baron Holland (1705-1772- the Secretary of State. Henry Fox was the father of Charles James Fox of later fame that resulted in the fall of "our Buckingham friends" i.e. Pitt and Co.
See W/27.

W/30 – May 18. 1756   Bath. Morgan's Coffee House

My dear Dell

I am sorry to sit down to give you so bad an account of our friend, Potter, but I am under the greatest apprehensions for him. He found himself considerably better the first week after his arrival, but is now relaps'd, and does not imagine he can hold out above a month longer. As the Parliament will rise in a week, I think the most prudent measure for me to take, is to make no hasty declaration, till I have felt the pulses of the most considerable people with you, for I shou'd not chuse (sic) an opposition of six month duration, tho' I shou'd laugh at one of a week. However in case of a vacancy, it wou'd be right that a general rumour of my standing shou'd be spread, that none of my friends might engage themselves. It is with great unwillingness I think of A but I am forc'd to the step. I think it impossible for P to recover, but he may languish a month. Now, Mr Surveyor, I have a favour to ask of you. It is that you wou'd make Cat Street a good road to the Parsonage, for I had much rather come that way then by Church Street. I wish the banks were brick'd in the upper part of the street, as you have lower down.

I have spent a very agreable (sic) ten days here, but the anxiety on poor Potter's account has hurt me very much. We have the best company here, a few wits and unaffected beauties, which I assure you are wonders in such a publick place. Colonel Crawford din'd with me here - Sir Hungerford Bland has been here about a fortnight – I intend a little tour into Wales next Sunday to see Mr Morris's and Chepstow etc. and then shall return to you.

I am dear Dell. Your affectionate humble servant   John Wilkes

My compliments to Mrs Dell, Mr Stephens and all our friends.
Morgan's Coffee House eleven. Goodnight.

The route to Prebendal House via Church Street is still narrow and the road on the corner of Parsons Fee and Castle or Cat Street was lowered in accordance with Wilkes' request. Potter's health continues to be a worry for Wilkes but he lingered on another three years.
Sir Hungerford Bland is probably John Peach Hungerford, the Member of Parliament for Leicester (1775-1790). Although not a Member of Parliament at this date and before he took the additional surname of Peach, their paths must have crossed socially. Indeed, then the son of a Yorkshire baronet, he was a fellow student of Mr Leeson at Leiden and a contemporary of Wilkes there in the mid 1740's.
Hungerford's subsequent Parliamentary career was one of compromise. Twenty years later, however, he supported Wilkes in Parliament when in 1775 he (Wilkes) called for an increase in representation for the growing number of large towns and the rooting out of rotten boroughs.

W/31 - Saturday Oct. 16. 1756   St James's Place

Dear Dell

Before I left Aylesbury, I got a lease of Jackson's garden for 21 years I am unwilling to lose this year, and am naturally impatient; so that I must desire you to make all my compliments to the Feoffees, and shou'd take it as a favour, if they wou'd grant my Brother a Lease of the garden late Jackson's, the house and garden of Ironmonger, the ground you mention 'd of Chilton, and the other slip almost opposite to your back gates. I mean to have Ironmonger my under tenant. I beg there may be a special meeting call'd and if it is agreable to the gentlemen, on Monday the 25th of this month, or the Tuesday and Wednesday following. Present my compliments to Mr Price, and tell him I shall esteem it a particular favour, if he will finish the Lease as soon as he can and transmit it to me here, and my Brother will immediately execute the counterpart, which I will bring down with me. My Brother's stile (style) is, Mr Heaton Wilkes, of St John's Square, Malt Distiller. I wou'd observe all usual covenants, and leave it to you and Mr Price: but I cannot tell you how much you will oblige me to get it done soon. As to Chilton, you must smooth him up, and I believe Ironmonger wants a little coaxing. I sent him some money by Thorpe. Pray desire Samuel to bottle off the porter and ale as soon as it is fit; for I shall want him to return with me, when I leave Aylesbury the next time. I leave Thorpe a great many men, and he sole director. Hope he looks well after them.

My best respects to Mrs Dell, Miss Sukey, Mr Stephens etc and believe me, Dear Dell

Yours sincere friend   John Wilkes

I wish you to digest well the plan of the Stone-bridge road. G G has it at heart and you would find it in turn to great account to yourself to gratify him in it. It is now eleven, goodnight. I wish Thorpe would write to me here what progress the men have made at A. I will be with you, whenever you summon me about the lease, and I hope it will not exceed the time I mention'd the 25th, 26th, or 27th. The lease for 21 years. I want hare and partridge, extremely for the next week, Mr Gamekeeper.

It fell to Wilkes' younger brother, Heaton to carry on the family distilling business. (Heaton was their mother's maiden name) and by involving his brother in Aylesbury affairs, perhaps Wilkes was trying to strengthen his family's hold on the town. G.G. was undoubtedly George Grenville, Pitt, the elder's brother-in-law, who was to hold various offices of state in later years. (See also W/32 re the Stonebridge).
Last mentioned eighteen months ago it is not clear whether the earlier offer (W/24) for Chilton's piece of land was accepted.

W/32 – Oct. 23. 1756 St James's Place

Dear Dell

I thank you very heartily for the zeal you show on every occasion to serve me. I beg you to hasten Mr Price as much as possible. I wish the Lease to be made out from last Michaelmas. I shall see Mr Grenville this morning, and will mention to him your thoughts of the Stone-bridge road. You are very short -sighted about my garden; but give me credit for so much taste, when I say even next year it will be infinitely better than ever; and you will think so too. I am greatly oblig'd to you for the partridges, and a brace of hares I receiv'd last night: but alas! What are these to my cravings? I hope to be with you next Wednesday evening, and be so kind as to order me a good fire, and a couple of fowls roasted for my supper. Tell Layland I have not time to write to her. My best compliments to Mrs Dell etc.

I am, Dear Dell

Yours sincere friend John Wilkes.
Within a week, Dell was negotiating about the lease but as a quid pro quo he had raised the matter with Wilkes of the Stone-bridge road for, as one of the Surveyors of the Highway, Dell was anxious for a bridge to be built over the river Thame on the Bicester Road out of town close to Quarrendon (or an existing one repaired). Wilkes' friend George Grenville had been pressing for this. Game is again on Wilkes' mind.

W/33 – Nov. 23.1756 St James's Place

Dear Dell

I enclose to you a note on Honeywood for £40, payable next Tuesday. I wrote yesterday to Mr Potter and told him my real sentiments of what will probably happen at A. You and I must be very cautious, least we burn our fingers, without doing him any good. Hitherto we have been victorious; but without the proper forces we must be defeated, if an enemy takes the field against us. Let me know if Potter writes to you, and be cautious in your answers to him, but tell him the whole truth. Let me hear by the return of the post, if the note comes safe to your hands, and in what humour my brother voters are. I wou'd do Potter all the service I cou'd but I wou'd not appear frantic in a cause in which I despair of success <u>against any opponent whatever</u>. I have seen Dr Milles, Potter's brother in law and he says he believes P is absolutely determin'd. If so, you and I will be laughed at as little as possible. I beg you to call on Price, and press him again about the Lease.

I fear, an election breeding ill blood, and <u>retarding</u> some at least some of my schemes. Is not the day of meeting yet fixed? I wish you from time to time to look in on my library, and see how Russell goes on. Pray tell Thorpe to finish in the front of the house as soon as he can; and Russell to point the hall door towards the churchyard <u>directly</u>. Since I wrote to you I have heard from P. He comes to town next Sunday, his seat will be vacated the middle of the week, and I fancy the writ out Saturday the 4th December, and the election Tuesday the 7th. It is not yet absolutely settled. Nothing is to be given, if beat by bribery, a petition and the C to determine it. I think all this perfectly senseless, and if the Merchant has a grain of sense himself, he cou'd never wish for such an opportunity. Think what a Parl. are to determine this Petition; for if an opposition comes, that will be the case. The new powers are but half established. Be cautious about every word you say to every creature, and always have it in mind that it will be reheard before the H. Do not let P suspect you know anything but what comes from him directly to you. I will get you the best directions for your conduct as Returning Officer; and on that account it becomes you not to be too principal in any management. I have sent you by this post the book of the voters, and beg you not to efface that but to make such another as soon as you can. I shall not probably be at A the whole time. I wish you to get handbills printed for my gates and chains, to be sold at your house. My name is not to be mentioned in them. It is done cheapest in Northampton.

I am, Dear Dell Your sincere friend John Wilkes

Not a word of this to any creature
This letter is a mixture of domestic, political and estate matters. Messrs Honeywood & Fuller were London bankers established in 1737 (177 Lombard Street) and by 1754 the firm was known as Honeywood, Fuller & Cope.

Wilkes is, as ever, cautious about Thomas Potter. Although willing to support him if he (Potter) decides to stand again. Wilkes is gloomy, however, of Potter succeeding "against any opponent whatever" On what does Wilkes base this remark? Does he imply that Potter is not able or willing to satisfy the Aylesbury electoral demands for a second term, the first having proved so expensive?

In 1747 Potter inherited the bulk of his father, John Potter, an Archbishop of Canterbury's fortune, said to be £70.000 to £90,000 but as subsequent events were to prove, Potter was aiming for high office and Aylesbury was merely a stepping-stone in his political ambitions.

This is the only mention of Wilkes' library in all the correspondence although it is clear that he is accumulating one at the Prebendal. The Russell family was involved in building and carpentry. When Wilkes library was sold at auction in 1764 there were nearly 950 items that raised a total of over £500. In 1802 his executors, in a similar operation, raised £742 from 1478 items. (Both sets of figures taken from Sale of Catalogues of Libraries of Eminent Persons. 1973)

W/34 Nov. 27. 1756 St James's Place

Dear Dell

I have had another letter from P full of the same absurb particulars I read to you to A but he says he had further scheme to communicate to me as soon as he sees me, which will be tomorrow night. A friend of mine was here yesterday and wou'd have got my leave to have come down to A with £1500 certainly to be spent, and wou'd take his chance: but I will listen to no offers, while P thinks of standing. I will remonstrate to P in the strongest terms how certainly he will ruin himself and me at A. You shall hear from me again on Tuesday. Nothing but gates and chain in our hand-bills. Let me beg you to call often on Price about the Lease. My compliments to Mrs Dell, Miss Sukey, Mr Stephens etc.

Your sincere friend. John Wilkes.

Bigg's is a good letter. I will take the first favourable opportunity to serve him

Word is out that someone has £1500 ready to be spent in bribes at the next election which in Wilkes' opinion will ruin him and Potter if they both stand and as the price spirals upwards.

W/35 – Dec. 2 1756 St James's Place

Dear Dell

I have just left poor P extremely ill, of the gout in his stomach I believe. He could not stir out on my account today, nor can he kiss hands yet; so it is quite uncertain when he will vacate his seat. I wish it may not be in the way you and I most dread. Shou'd that be the case, I am infallibly your candidate; but I hope better things for myself, for you, for the public.

Strut of Breme's Court, Chancery Lane, shall bring you a written account of what is legally to be done; but I will be with you as soon as anything happens. On no account be concern'd in any unwarrantable favours bestowed on any body. I suspect a snake in the grass and that P will be opposed from the Shannon. He thinks himself secure, and is therefore too careless. I will write to you the first opportunity.

Yours sincere friend

John Wilkes

Let me hear from you by the next post.

Wilkes is preparing for the worse with regard to Potter's health although the latter had by now been appointed Joint Vice-Treasurer of Ireland. He recovered and survived another two years. Although content to serve for Aylesbury, he is hinting of "better things" and that Potter's candidature might be challenged from the Irish faction.

W/36 – Jan. 27. 1757 St James's Place

Dear Dell

I have great suspicion that the present Parl. is not very long liv'd. I must therefore keep a good lookout, and be well prepar'd, if a great event should happen to-morrow. If you can without much suspicion get me list of all those who took any charity, within the last twelvemonth, I shou'd be greatly obliged to you. I must not be suspected much, till I have open'd myself to the Reg. I am now on the best of terms with him, and have every other post obliging letters from him. You make use of Potter's name in the enquiry, as if he intends to stand again, shou'd anything happen. Let me beg you to make another list, digested in the same clever way the other was, and as accurate as possible. The former is lost or it would have help'd you very much. Do not hurry yourself, nor lose any time of leisure. I long much to know the present temper of the Borough; I wrote to young Burnham to get evidence against the persons who broke Spurs' windows, and intend to move the Court of King's Bench against them. B is not to mention my name. Potter quite approves and will bring me one of the guinea causes to a hearing. My compliments to Mrs Dell and all friends
I am, Dear Dell, your sincere friend

John Wilkes

I am in great want of game.

Talk of the Government collapsing is still ripe and Dell is being warned to prepare in his usual efficient manner a Who's Who in voting patterns. Sir Francis Dashwood of West Wycombe, the county's Militia Commander in Chief, is probably being referred to when Wilkes says he has open'd himself to the Regiment i.e. advised of his intention of standing. The Reg(iment), however, could just as easily refer to his support already in Parliament.

W/37 – Feb. 3 1757 St James's Place

Dear Dell

I thank you much for your letter, and the game, which proved excellent. I think the chain very well sold, and I wish Hickman cou'd help me to as good a chap for the gates and the old iron. I long to know what answer you have had from old Chilton. I take it for granted he curses me very heartily. Pity the Justice had not been on the spot to have made him pay. I wou'd give him and his Wife, or the longest liver £12 a year, and a few guineas in pocket for the purchase, or £150. Walker is in town and is to come to me next Sunday morning. I will ask him about certificates etc. I shall see P today, and will tell me about Ray. As everything is now finish'd, do not let us lose with P the merit of such services by complaints tho' never so just. You certainly must see this is sound policy. Adieu.

Your sincere friend   John Wilkes

You shall have the list of voters objected to by P when I come into the country. It is lock'd up in my bureau. Pray tell Mr St I wish to hear from him as soon as it suits him. My compliments to all our friends.

More domestics mixed with more equally obscure ones. Wilkes is still involved with Chilton and his property but this time the Justices seem to have become involved.

W/10 –Tuesday April 19 (1757) St James's Place

Dear Dell

In the first place I am to tell you what is uppermost in my thoughts, that every favourable sympton (sic) has hitherto attended my dear girl; secondly I think nothing shou'd as yet be done to your barn, for as we have now a pretty good chance of getting Chilton's house, the tiles from thence will at once make a compleat (sic) job of it. If you cannot get it under, I will give the most extravagant price of £200 sooner than be without it. Let me desire you to get me the arch, and the new brew-house completed as soon as you can. I wish to know what justices you have at the quarter sessions, and what business is done there. How does the affair of the churchwardens go on, and what new speeches you have had from your great orator Bass or the amiable Hemp Horrard. I wish you to consult the women, especially your good wife, about the new place for washing and ironing, as well as brewing. I wou'd have it compleat as we can without a german stove, etc and I can very well spare the room above, over the new coach house and stabling, is sufficient room for all lumber. Let me beg you to get finish'd, if possible, in a fortnight, and all the rubbish moved out of the yard. I think to keep a few milk white bantams by way of weeders; but no other fowls, except peacocks, who will survive even Stephens's execrations.

The city are in the greatest uproar about the removal of Mr Pitt; and Byng's affair is luckily already forgot. Potter's daughter has the small pox very bad in the natural way; but is now recovering. My compliments to Mrs Dell and all friends.

Yours John Wilkes

Now that daughter Polly's attack of small pox was thought to have eased, Wilkes is able to think of other matters. The Chilton affair rumbles on and Wilkes' offer has risen to £200. He is also doing his best to improve the domestic arrangements at his Aylesbury home even to the extent of asking Dell's wife for advice as to seemingly mundane matters such as washing and ironing and German stoves.

William Pitt the Elder's dismissal in April by King George the Second led to eleven weeks in which no administration was in place. Matters were only resolved when the Duke of Newcastle resumed the position of First Lord of the Treasury and formed a new administration on the understanding that Pitt served as Secretary of State. This was the background to the "uproar" to which Wilkes refers. The Byng affair is, of course, the news of Admiral Byng's court-marshal for neglect of duty and subsequent execution.

John Bass is referred to in W/13 and W/18 as " the great orator", but not to be invited to any rout as he was not considered an Independent. He was probably a baker of this name who died in 1765.

The amiable Hemp Horrard (alias William Horwood) was a hemp dresser of Aylesbury who married Mary Oviatts at Cuddington in 1738. He died in 1762.

W/38 – April 26 1757

Dear Dell

I am very much oblig'd to you for your letter of yesterday, and for the anxiety you express for my dear girl. She is in as fine a way as can be. All the symptoms favourable. She is pretty full, but not above a dozen on her face. Nothing can be conceived more patient and good-humoured than she has been the whole time. I had desired her Mother to attend her before, and after the inoculation <u>was</u> perform'd. I wrote to Mrs Wilkes recommending Miss Wilkes to her Mother's care; but she has never once come near her. I am greatly oblig'd to my Mother Wilkes etc. for their daily care. I desire it may continue to rain in still to your barn till the brew house and arch are finish'd. You last reason about the pleas is excellent, all the rest trash. I suppose you will repair the roof over the racks, where the hay was put down. I shou'd think it ought to be one uniform ceiling, but I leave the whole to your care; I only wish it done very speedily. I shall bring Miss Wilkes to Aylesbury, when her last physicking is over.   I am very glad you had no quarter sessions, to shew the importance of every one of us justices. How you longed for the Aylesbury Justice? Let me know from time to time what is done in relations to the church-warden. My particular compliments to Mr Bell, when you see him. Every thing here relating to the Ministry is in confusion; and no judgement can be form'd as to the event. My respects to all friends with you. I am Dear Dell

Your affectionate, humble servant John Wilkes

No partridges to taste of the green corn! alas! alas!

Wilkes' concern for his daughter, Polly's attack of smallpox is heightened by the apparent lack of interest taken by his wife, Mary. His appeals for her to attend the sick bed have apparently gone unanswered and he has been forced to fall back on Mother Wilkes help. A formal deed of separation followed.

Although the ministry is said to be in confusion, there is nothing to indicate it will fall and trigger an election. Dell. as a tenant of Wilkes is looking for the repair of his barn by the landlord. (See also W/10) but other domestic matters seem to have greater priority at this time.

W/39 – May 3.1757   St James's Place

Dear Dell

You may now congratulate me on my dear girl's being past all danger. She has gone thro' that most malignant distemper amazingly well, and is now in the course of physick which prudentially followed it. She longs to be at Aylesbury and we begin to prepare. I mean Polly and I for you will scarcely see her Mother there in summer, whatever you do in autumn. I entirely approve of your selling the rack and manger to James Lee at Hickman's appraisement, and I would not take the money, but have it sett off in my bill. As you mention that we have not old bricks enough, I wou'd do nothing about the Arch; but wish to get everything clear'd away as soon as you can. As soon as you have finish'd the brew-house, Thorpe may make two brewings of 12 bushels each. I have heard you farmers often complain of the quantities of your corn destroyed by partridges. Now therefore in breeding time is the season to do you justice, and pray send me up some of the destroyers. You are very merry with the modesty of an Aylesbury poacher, which I hold to be the equal to a prime minister's honesty or a bishop's religion. Have you no borough news to send me? My compliments to Mrs Dell and all our friends

Yours John Wilkes

More domestic chit-chat but the Good News is that daughter, Polly is out of danger and they are preparing to spend the summer at Aylesbury.

W/40 – May 12 1757 St James's Place

Dear Dell

I thank you for your letter of the 8th, and your kind congratulations on my dear girl's recovery; She continues very well, but has not yet finished her physicking, on account of a little rash she has had which is neither an unusual nor a bad sympton . I desire you to offer the rack and manger to Mr Bell as a present from me, and tell him how glad I am it suits his conveniency. This will ingratiate you too not a little with him; but if he refuses to accept it, you must get Hickman to settle it with him, and for him to take the money, which would not do at all either for you or me. Your new church-wardens seem already to be possessed of all the insolence of office. They will be disappointed however, as well as the old ones, for I shall not be in the country till the time limited for laying the information is expir'd, as I remember the act. I rejoice the Blues are going. I suffer more from that inconvenience than any of you. How does my garden look? Are you yet reconcil'd to the alterations? Miss Wilkes came here last Saturday, and I have two maid servants solely to tend her; one of which will come with me into the country. She will not have a single scar. I am to give you her compliments, and she longs to see Betsy. Adieu.

Your most humble servant.   John Wilkes

Betsy (Elizabeth) was probably Dell eldest daughter b.1753 who was a couple of years younger than Wilkes' daughter, Polly. They must have played together as children when Wilkes and his family were resident at Prebendal House.

W/12 – Saturday 28 May (1757) Great George St

Dear Dell

I intended to have been this week at Aylesbury, but am prevented by business of consequence. I shall certainly come to you this day sevennight, and I intent to give you a grand supper, not dinner, as it is market day, and a rout for the Town, in the usual manner. I shall not come until about six; and shall dine at Blackwell's. I am proud to know that my worthy constituents approve me. I am here caress'd in a manner, which does me the truest honour. I mean to give the supper at the White Hart, and pray speak to Hill accordingly. Pray tell Dr Stephens my intention, and invite to supper at eight all the independents. You remember that Saturday is the King's birthday.

I am ever, your affectionate friend. John Wilkes

If any persons are disposed to meet me, let it be only a mile or two from town.

Edward Blackwell was mine host at the White Hart, Great Missenden where many-stayed overnight en route from London but the proposed supper was at the hostelry of the same name in Aylesbury. One way of welcoming a popular figure into town was for them to be carried or chaired. These days, of course, it is on an open top bus!

W/13 – Tuesday 31 May (1757) Great George Street

Dear Dell

I have the favour of your letter of 30th May (yesterday) and beg you invite all the independents (therefore no Jack Bass) to sup with Mr Wilkes on Saturday evening at seven or eight, as they like best. Pray desire Mr Hill to let us have a good supper. I will give a rout, and will bring you bank or cash, as you like for it. I am sure that I am following the true interest of this kingdom, and I know that you will approve, when I see you. I am, with my compliments to all friends, Dear Dell

Yours sincere friend   John Wilkes

Things are hotting-up in Aylesbury and support for Wilkes is being elicited from the Independents by way of a rout at Hill's White Hart in Aylesbury. Bass is also referred to in W/10 and W/18

W/11 – Tuesday 21 May (1757) (The date and day of the week of this letter does not coincide) St James's Place

Dear Dell

I have only time to tell you that all C.T. said on Sunday is true. I have seen Potter. He is Vice Treasurer of Ireland but has not yet kiss'd hands. He seems inclined to offer himself again at Aylesbury, but is to give me his definite answer tomorrow morning at nine. I have been explicit with him that he can never be elected again at Aylesbury, but if he stands, I will not oppose him. I have not time to give you reasons. Be on your guard, and pray do not go from home an hour; I mean out of town. Goodnight eleven

Potter's appointment to government office heralds his resignation at Aylesbury followed by re-election here or elsewhere, so all is on hold in the borough. C.T. may well be Charles Townshend (1725-67), a contemporary of Wilkes at Leiden University who was a dazzling but unreliable politician who nevertheless became Chancellor of the Exchequer in 1766.

W/14 – Wednesday June 22. (1757) St James's Place

Dear Dell

I have been this morning with Mr Potter, and he entirely relinquishes to me your good borough of Aylesbury. I expect he will in a very few days kiss hands for the place of Vice-Treasurer of Ireland. I am determined to offer my services and will give two guineas per man, with the promise of whatever more anyone else offers. Let me beg you to be prepar'd and digest thoroughly the whole plan. Potter offers to come down, and act any part we wou'd have him, either by openly espousing me, or by a mock fight against me. I am secure of no opposition to me either from Fox or Newcastle. I am ready here as soon as ever P kisses hands. Let everything be a profound secret. If you think two guineas is not enough, I will offer 3, or even 5, to be secure.

I am Dear Dell

Your sincere friend.   John Wilkes

Potter has at last confirmed that he has relinquished the borough upon his appointment to government and is about to kiss hands upon his appointment – the formal acknowledgement by the monarch but in his own good time. The bidding for votes has started at two guineas a man "even five to be secure."

W/15 – Thursday June 23. 1757 St James's Place

Dear Dell

I believe in two or three days I shall open the campaign at Aylesbury. P is not yet return'd and no time is yet fixed for kissing hands. I have seen Charles L. He is strong with me, and gives me letters accordingly. He advises 3 guineas a man. If you are of the same opinion, I will not hesitate. It is a kind of retainer, or fee at entrance. I have wrote this post to Walker at Oxford, and to Sir W Stanhope but recommending secrecy. Let nothing transpire. I intend Tom Smith for a principal agent. I hope in all cases to have the start, and am determined to carry my point. Be attentive to every whisper. Adieu. I suppose you had my letter by Sherif

Wilkes was a little premature the previous day in W/14 for Potter has not yet kissed hands to confirm the appointment. Charles L(owndes) is believed to be strongly on Wilkes' side and gives letters of approval accordingly. The price has already levelled-out at three guineas a man and is described as a "kind of retainer or fee at entrance" – a euphemism if ever there was one.

There is a suggestion that another agent is being groomed as Dell is now Constable as well as Returning Officer; the latter was a sinecure in the hands of Prebendal Manor of which Wilkes was the lord.

W/2 – Monday (1757) This letter is approximately in sequence

Dear Dell

I send you the two last books made out for the good Borough. W at last has gone out in a stink - I always despis'd such an opponent - Ellis will lend 5, and I think at present of 4, and in a very few days - pray with Smith, and Bob Neale, and Parish Books - make me out a list of all you think worthy of my charity, to whom you wou'd have me really give as soon as possible; and you may send it to me in two or three covers safely by the post, or by the coach according to which is the first conveyance –Pray mention when Mr Liptrap's house is fitt for his reception – Does my 40 pounds worth of half crowns do me sixpenny worth of good? Goodnight.

The pressure on Edward Willes especially with regard to the projected cost of the election has forced him to withdrew his attempt to be elected and is reflected in this comment "W has gone out in a stink." This remark proved to be premature as Willes did not get the job that would have forced him to vacate the seat. (A Member of Parliament who took office was obliged to resign and seek re-election). Matters seem to be coming to a head with the price of a vote settling down between four and five (guineas).

Wilkes, by asking about who is worthy of his "charity", is assessing the total possible liability from all quarters of the town. Those in receipt of parish relief are listed in the parish books and consequently forfeit their right to vote as potwallers.

The following three letters between the sitting member, Thomas Potter and John Wilkes are inserted here for continuity in the build-up to Wilkes' Aylesbury campaign. They do not form part of the series of letters between Wilkes and Dell

Tuesday June 28. 1757

A liberty to resign the Borough of Aylesbury into your hands.

I most heartily wish you a safe and cheap election at Aylesbury and shld with great pleasure contribute towards it if I had any interest to contribute. I kiss hands with the rest tomorrow and then my seat is vacant but most unfortunately the new writ cannot occur 'til next Tuesday … you should employ some careful person in Town to speak to the messenger of the Great Seal, Mr Crawford who if he is told that he will receive ten guineas will ride so as to deliver the writ to the Under Sheriff that evening at Aylesbury and then if the Under Sheriff attends and has his precept ready, you may before the sun sets proclaim the election for Saturday morning. By this means you will avoid two inconveniences – the seditious conversations of the Market people on Saturday and the day of leisure for hatching iniquity. Sunday I would myself undertake the settling with Crawford but that leave London on Friday morning.

29 June. 1757

I will take care to order the writ for Aylesbury that evening for Wednesday morning. I think therefore you had better not make any declaration until Saturday morning and if you give a rout that evening and promise to distribute money on Monday I shld hope you will keep things quiet. Mr Pitt has done what he could to prevent the D of Newcastle sending down any opposition to you and from every other quarter you have no reason to expect one.

Friday 1 July. 1757

Pray direct a line to me at Bath to inform me of the success of yr election. I have saved you a scouring at least I hope from Admiral Knowles whom by great accident I met with his bags in his chaise ready to set out for A if the D of Newcastle did not forbid him. I talked to him in such a manner that he promised me to carry his bags home again.

Admiral Sir Charles Knowles was member of Parliament between 1749-52 for the pocket borough of Galton in Surrey (with 22 electors). He was clearly looking around for another seat in an effort to advance his career but clearly failed in this.

W/41 – Jan. 3 1758 Great George Street

Dear Dell

I rejoice that you are in such good spirits - I hope my other worthy voters are the same - however you will hear me thunder out my complaints for the want of game – my little angel too squeaks out (tho' thank heaven not so bad as Ned Willes) that she thought she had been a favourite with Mr Dell, but not a bird from him all these holydays – you must then, (to make peace, Mr Constable), get me a brace of Partridges to be directed to Miss Wilkes and to come up by Friday's coach: I come to Aylesbury Thursday evening and stay there till Sunday morning - a thousand thanks for your turkey and chince, which were excellent - I must beg you to compromise matters about the new Surveyor, so that I may have no squabble at Wendover. If you undertake to mend Walton St in the course of the next year, perhaps that would satisfy Price and every body; but settle it in the manner most agreeable to yourselves, and either let me take the first two in your list (which is legal) or let that rule be broke thro' by consent – you are clever, and know the consequences of these trifling quarrels; therefore put an early stop to them - Heaven bless you.

Your affectionate John Wilkes

Having now become one of Aylesbury's Members of Parliament albeit without any ballot or contest, Wilkes has returned to domestic matters.

W/42 – Jan. 21 1758 Great George St

Dear Dell

I beg you not to be under such violent apprehensions what to do securely with the immense sums Fountain may bring you. You may keep them till I return to Aylesbury; and may sleep very soundly under the roof with them. F is a rogue and when I have a little leisure in spring, I shall consult you how to get rid of him at once, which I can do easily since Mrs Astley's death, as the whole estate is now mine. When I see Williams and Price at Easter, I will endeavour to get Hickman's business done. I beg you to remind me of it. Yesterday we voted in the committee £100.000 to subsist and keep together the Han(*overian*) Army for the present. My best compliments to Mrs Dell, and all our friends. My dear girl is return'd perfectly well to Chelsea. Pray thank Mr Stephens for his fine venison.

I am, Dear Dell, your affectionate friend.

John Wilkes

What is the money given into his keeping that Dell is worried about? As the election is over it can't be a "war chest" to bribe the voters so it must relate to a domestic matter. Fountain is probably Thomas Fountain of Brickhill. The Marriage Settlement between Wilkes and Miss Mary Mead(e) dated 21 May 1747 included 200 acres known as Eaton Leys in Great Brickhill. Under the will of Wilkes' mother-in-law, Mary Mead(e), who was the widow of John Mead(e), a wealthy London grocer, she bequeathed a sixth share in Eaton Leys to Ann Astley for her lifetime. Her recent death, referred to by Wilkes, has finally released the whole of the estate to him. Miss Astley in her will asked to be buried at Soulbury, in Buckinghamshire. " near to the Mead family."

W/43 – Feb. 28 1758 Great George Street

Dear Dell

I only take up the pen to congratulate you and Mrs Dell on the happy increase of your family, and to ease your mind of your friendly concern for me. I assure you I have not lost five guineas these six months, and you know I have gain'd (by mortality) some hundreds, Returning Officers etc. paid. Never disturb yourself with idle reports. Time is the great comforter of this kind of lie. Sir W.H. told me Terry mentioned to him and he laughed at it. These things hurt Merchants, not Gentlemen, at least like me, who do not, to my knowledge, owe six pence at A, or elsewhere, except the current expense of the week. I shall be very glad to see you here. You will find a warm house, and a warmer reception from

Your affectionate friend.   John Wilkes

If anything happens to Wm S, let me have a line.

John and Elizabeth Dell's daughter, Mary was baptised at Aylesbury 21 February 1758. Her date of birth in the register was given as 27 March in the previous year. Wilkes, as was often the custom in those days, has refrained from mentioning the girl by name before as her baptism had not taken place. (There was a superstition prevailing at that time concerning an unbaptised child. It was considered unwise to mention him or her by name before baptism for fear that the devil might take the child for his own).

Has Dell been chastising his friend over financial imprudence?

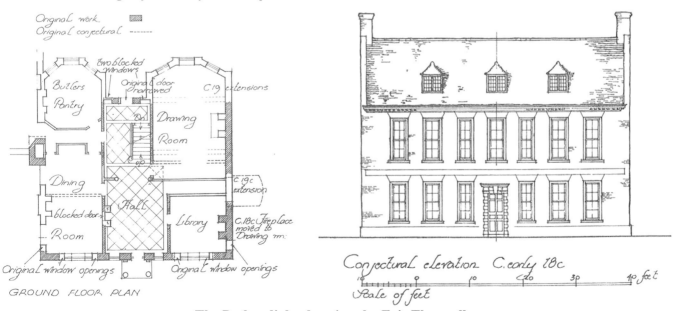

The Prebendial – drawings by Eric Throssell

W/44 – April 1 1758   Great George Street

Dear Dell

As the time for the nomination of the Overseers of the Poor of our good County Town approaches, I wish you to take into your thorough consideration that growing evil of the poor themselves. Unless something effectual is done, it bids fair to ruin you and most of the other parishes in England. Smith was with me for an hour this week, and I find he has some scheme to offer. I wish heartily the parish wou'd agree with him, for I am persuaded it would be by far their cheapest manner, and the poor wou'd not be then supported in idleness, as they now are. I come to Aylesbury Thursday noon, and stay with you till Sunday. On Saturday we hold a Petty Sessions. Whatever agreement cou'd be made with Smith, by general consent, the new Overseer might then agree to, and Revett and I wou'd ratify it on the spot. Mr Bell must be first consulted, and Mr Hall etc. I mean before it comes to be propos'd in Vestry. My best compliments attend Mrs Dell etc. My dear girl sends hers. She is perfectly well and in high spirits.

Your most affectionate friend , John Wilkes

Wilkes broaches for the first time in these letters the subject of the poor in the borough,"the growing evil of the poor themselves" as he puts it. Unless something effective is done it is likely to ruin Aylesbury and most other parishes in England. He complains that they (the poor) are being supported in idleness – a claim echoed down the centuries – but quite what scheme Smith has to offer is not revealed. Tom Smith was the appointed Aylesbury's Overseer of the Poor.

W/45 – May 2 1758   Great George Street

Dear Dell

With your letter came likewise a letter from Mr Matthias Dagnall to acquaint me with Mr Williams's Death and that the surviving Trustee had been long under an engagement to continue the succession in the same line, whose ancestors the Donor thought at first agreeable. They had therefore unanimously pitched on Mr Archdale Williams etc etc. I am forced to acquiesce, and have accordingly wrote to Dagnall. I come the 13th and stay till the 22nd. The school election is on the 20th and I hope you will contrive the Feoffees in Whitsun week Who you like.
Goodnight, eleven

News of Mr W(ilson) Williams's death at Bath, a Harding Trustee since 1736 and an Aylesbury apothecary, has been conveyed to Wilkes who has been forced to agree to Archidale, William's son being appointed in his place. There was a long tradition that the appointment of Trustees should follow along family lines.   (One of the original Trustees named in the Founder's Will was a Thomas Williams, father of Wilson, who died in 1732). The Dagnalls were stationers in Aylesbury for several generations.
Wilkes is also anxious to attend the meeting of the board of the newly formed Foundling Hospital.

W/46 – Sept. 8 1758 Kirby over Carr

Dear Dell

I have only the melancholy new to tell you, Mr Returning Officer, and the other worthy electors of the County Town, that one of your members is in perfect health, and so is I can assure you your most gracious Sovereign - I am here at a most worthy divine's. Mr Davidson's, who treats me with two things I infinitely love, chearful (sic) company and excellent hock – Judge if I am likely soon to decamp – I talk however of penetrating into Scotland, if I can persuade my good host. I suspect however I shall not succeed in this, as I never heard of any of its natives returning thither - I have another good piece of news to tell you, that I have wrote to Mr Stephens, to desire him to get me good standard apricocks (sic), haut-boys etc. for fruit in Chiltons close - That ground lies so convenient for me, I must have it for fruit, and the whole next year; therefore do not grumble, only look grave and charge me with the whole expense of the new wall etc. I have no objection to hiring or purchasing any other piece of ground for you, but you must not set your wicked heart on this, nor Brookes neither for a staddle. Do not be angry, I shall contrive some other way to make you amends.

I am, Dear Dell

Yours sincere and affectionate friend. John Wilkes

Wilkes is in one of his jocular moods when he talks of "penetrating" into Scotland and, as in the next (W/47), his apparent aversion to Scotland and its people is surfacing; or is it all jest? Chilton's piece of land so close or part of Wilkes' property is almost becoming an obsession. Is it that he wants the old butcher to give up his lease for payment? How otherwise does one get rid of unwanted tenants? The use of the word staddle in this context is thought to mean support from elsewhere.

W/47 – Sept. 26 1758 Edinburgh

Dear Dell

I hope before you open'd this letter, you took the necessary precaution of airing it, drying it by the fire etc., and washing your own hands in vinegar, for fear of a propagations of some Scotch animals in our good County town. I would not have wrote to you from hence but to tell you I am informed Sir H.P .intends to sell by auction the whole family estate in Aylesbury. If it shou'd be so, I may contrive to purchase the whole, and I beg you to get me all the information you can. I intend to return to Aylesbury, before I go to London; and spend a fortnight among my good friends, in the way you have recommended to me. If the weather grow bad, I shall return in a few days. To morrow I go on horseback to the Duke of Argyle. I am with   my compliments to Mrs Dell and all friends, Dear Dell. your sincere friend

John Wilkes

In this whimsical, some would say downside offensive, slur on the Scots, Wilkes is displaying certain contempt towards their nation over and beyond his usual bantering tone.

News has reached him that the whole of the Packington family estate in Aylesbury may be going to auction and is seeking up-to-date information from Dell who is on the spot. His aim, which of course was not fulfilled, is to "continue to purchase the whole." This implies he has already purchased portions of the estate. The proposed sale of the Packington estate, which Wilkes was anxious to acquire, came to nothing at this stage. See also W/53. It was not until 1801 that Sir John sold the manor and estate to George, Marquis of Buckingham.

W/48 Nov. 16 1758 Great George Street

Dear Dell

I always take a pleasure in giving due praises to those, who merit them so well as my gamekeeper and tenant at the County Town of Bucks. It is likewise a hint to them to proceed, in so good a course. A haslet puts one in mind of a hog, but let me beg you not to send all that are due to me here at once, for fear I swear again the devil's in the swine. I think the affair of Oviat's license had better be dropp'd, if he can in any how do without a Spirituous Liquors License for this year. The thing is so illegal, and opens a door to so much future fraud from this precedent, that I wish it over, and no talk of it, for fear of informations against the poor fellow - I would pay the first - Few members are yet come to town - Most of those I have convers'd with are for preventing the Distillery's working for the next year, to secure a very good stock, and I fancy that opinion will prevail. If any thing new occurs, I beg you to write to me, and believe me ever

Yours sincere friend, John Wilkes

My dear girl perfectly well.

This is a hidden warning to Dell about a local licensing matter. Whatever Dell is proposing has not met with Magistrate Wilkes' approval at Quarter Sessions level but which distillery is involved nor the proposal, is not known. Oviats, at the centre of the concern, is a local victualler who at a later date was endeavouring to use a copyhold messuage in Silver Lane as a brew house. Perhaps it was a matter before the Manorial court pending a ruling.

W/49 – Nov. 21 1758 Great George Street

Dear Dell

I have signed the License and the Recognizance as you desire. I wou'd advise you to make use of the mediation of Mr Pugh, if he will undertake to get them sign'd, as perhaps from his great good nature he may ask it as a favour of Mr R. For my part, I have too much pride to consent that my name shou'd be made use of to him. I wish you to mention in your next, when the Christmas Quarter Sessions begin; that I may contrive to be with you then, and hold a Petty Sessions in the same week. Let me beg you to be attentive to every thing that passes at A. It is a very critical time. I dare not write more, but you guess to what this alludes.
Adieu, your affectionate friend

John Wilkes

My compliments to Mrs Dell & all friends

More local administrative matters are in hand and warranting discussion probably in Wilkes' capacity as a local magistrate. Why this is a critical time when only recently elected as Aylesbury's Member of Parliament is not clear. The Revd. William Pugh was a master at the Aylesbury Grammar School and curate at St Mary's.

W/50 – Dec. 23 1758 Great George Street

Dear Dell

I enclose to you two notes for £25 each which you will be so good as to turn into cash, and pay it to Smith. Let me know, if they come safe. You may tell Tom Bigg, that I have a promise of a First Lieutenancy for him in a very short time. I enclose to you a letter from young Argles, which I beg you to speak to him about as you think most proper in my name. Smith need not wait to write to me, but may go on in the way he judges will be most acceptable to our good friends. My dear girl is perfectly well, and is everything I wish her. The compliments of this merry season to you and Mrs Dell, not forgetting Sukey's fire-side.

I am, Dear Dell, your affectionate friend .

John Wilkes

This is another domestic missive. Tom Smith's appointment as Overseer of the Poor is imminent or already occurred.

W/52 – Feb. 17 1752 Great George St

Dear Dell

I had the pleasure of your letter, and shall be oblig'd to you, if you will mention to my Brother Trustees of Harding's Trust, how kindly I should take it, if they would consent to let Mr Edmonds have the vacant farm. I will take care of the other particulars you mention. Be so good to call on Mr Edmonds, and let him know he has me entirely with him, and that I wish him success. I have only time to add that I am, with my best compliments to Mrs Dell and all friends.

Your affectionate, humble servant

John Wilkes

My dear girl and I are much oblig'd for the game. Tell our good Parson there will be an additional tax on tobacco, therefore let them smoak (sic) away, while they can <u>so cheap</u>

Wilkes is seeking his fellow trustees of the Harding Charity agreement to Mr Edmonds taking a lease on one of their vacant farms. This is probably William Edmonds whose daughter Sarah (1736-1765) was the first wife of William Rickford Senior, grocer and tallow chandler. The lease does not appear to have materialised.
He also warns of an impending additional tax on tobacco and tells Dell's brother-in-law parson to "smoak away" while they are so cheap.

W/53 May 8 1759 Great George Street

Dear Dell

I thank you for your letter, and the intelligence it contains relating to the sale of the Packington estate. I must not appear too forward, but I long much to make the purchase and it is a purchase worth more to me than any other person whatever. Be so good to transmit to me from time to time all particulars you hear relating to it. I suppose it will be sold at fair auction. The road bill will certainly miscarry this Sessions. Have my good voters forgiven me the appointing of Tom Smith Overseer, and what did you do at Vestry about letting the Poor? Our wings are clipp'd as to the first reception of children in the different counties, but my scheme for Aylesbury goes on just the same as I first propos'd it; the writings are making , and the money order'd. I shall be in Aylesbury the beginning of June, and then we shall go about the repairs, and alterations etc. I am, Dear Dell

Yours affectionately, John Wilkes

Tom Smith has been appointed Overseers of the Poor which, from all accounts, is not a popular one. (See W/44 on Smith's thoughts about the poor). The establishment of a branch of the London Foundling Hospital continues to have Wilkes' attention and plans are being formulated. See also W/47 concerning the sale of the Packington estate. No Vestry records have survived to clarify what transpired at this meeting.

W/54 – May 15 1759 Great George Street

Dear Dell

I congratulate you on being elected a Governor of the Foundling Hospital, and of our Buckinghamshire Committee. Our purchase of Mr Lowndes will be finish'd this week. I shall be in Aylesbury on the second of June, and Mr Lowndes comes to me for some days in Whitsun week, to settle every thing relating to the building, or repairs, which we shall get finish'd as soon as possible. Mr Hill is chose a Governor. Our Committee meet on the 9th of June, and we shall then settle everything for the workmen to immediately to proceed. We mean directly to have no children under our care. Is any thing more done in relation to the letting of the poor? I beg my compliments to all friends, and am, Dear Dell
Your affectionate friend.   John Wilkes

The work of establishing the Foundling Hospital in Aylesbury is progressing and Hill from the White Hart has been made a Governor. The Crofts, which was a farmhouse in Walton, has been purchased from Mr Lowndes and is in the process of being converted. It is not clear whether the property was sold by William Lowndes, who was himself a Governor of Christs Hospital and the Westminster Infirmary, or his father Charles Lowndes of Chesham, a Secretary to the Treasury. William was a Captain in the Bucks Militia for 13 years.

W/55 – Aug. 25 1759 Great George Street

Dear Dell

I have order'd a buck to Aylesbury to be there to day, and if it has come, I wish you to call on Mr Hill at the White Hart, and desire him to get dinner on Tuesday next for all the independent voters. I shall return that morning and wish dinner was ready by one. Be so good to call on Smith, and settle with him the persons who are to be invited, for if one is omitted, he is a certain enemy. All the rest I leave to you, only let me beg you to invite Mr Bell and Mr Pugh with Mr Rowland, yourself, as soon as you certainly hear of the venison's being come. I am ever

Your affectionate

John Wilkes
Tom Smith was the newly appointed Overseer of the Poor and William Pugh a master at the Grammar School and curate of St Mary's.

W/56 – Oct. 11. 1759 *Great George Street*

Dear Dell

I suppose you so busy, in the little repair doing at my leanto, that you have not leisure to write till that is finish'd. Be so good to give me a line when it is done. I hope every thing is settled on a right footing as to the Foundling Hospital. I have sent Bob Neale money for Dancer's weekly expenses, and shall supply him from time to time. I hope very soon to get money from the Hospital to discharge all the tradesmen's bills. I wish you to take a greater lead there than you do at present. I see else that the power necessarily following the distribution of money, will be in hands I do not desire to see it in. I trust that before midsummer, the number of children will be more than doubled, by fitting up the barn etc. Consequently more money circulating, more dependence created etc. I can never myself attend it, but I have set the machine going. You may keep it in the right tract (sic) - I mean to confine Thorpe to two men in constant pay, besides Jack. This will reduce my garden to a certainty of no less than £82.1s.6d. per year besides seeds etc. allowing to Thorpe and Jack 9d. per day board wages - This regulation to take place from about April next, for in the meantime I think it may be cheaper manag'd. Let me know your sentiments on these matters, and believe me.

Very much yours   John Wilkes

This is another estate briefing coupled with instructions about the establishment of the Aylesbury Branch of the Foundling Hospital. Dell is being urged to take a "greater lead" in its administration which Wilkes can never attend to from London. Having set up the project, he desires those on the spot to keep it on track.

Tradesman's' bills are clearly building-up and Wilkes wants to retain overall control of finances rather than pass into other hands. He is hopeful of funds coming from the main organisation in London. Reading between the lines, however, Dell is not keen to be more closely involved for fear of becoming personally responsible for the finances. He had been already made a Trustee of the Hospital in 1755 and seems to be fully employed with the repairs to Prebendal – Wilkes' little" lean to", as he puts it.

The fate of the short lived Foundling Hospital in Aylesbury is outside the scope of this exercise but has been fully discussed in the late Mr Lloyd-Hart's splendid book 'John Wilkes and the Foundling Hospital'

W/57 – Oct. 30 1759   Great George Street

Dear Dell

I have settled my garden on so good a footing, that I shall not ever, I believe, consent to your favourite alteration of putting up the gates, even tho' it would now be an alteration. On the contrary I wish you cou'd sell my gates for me. The great man you name is not really tedious, but dangerous; yet I think we are pretty secure. I am sure if not of this, of one more to your advantage soon; but I believe you will have this - I cannot lend you my pew, tho' I would willingly assist your piety - I will tell you the particular reason (which you cannot guess) when I see you - I am very much obliged to you for the game, which was excellent - My father and I talk of Bristol at the end of the week. Nothing however absolutely fix'd. I beg my compliments to Mrs Dell, and all your family and am, Dear Dell,

Yours sincerely   John Wilkes

Whilst only a tenant of Wilkes, Dell is anxious to become a pew holder at St Mary's but his request to occupy it when Wilkes is not resident at the Prebendal is refused. As usual Wilkes hints at matters that are likely to affect the status quo that he cannot reveal until they meet up. Secrecy, or the need for it, is as ever Wilkes' way of keeping his subordinates guessing.

W/58 – Nov. 24 1759   Great George Street

Dear Dell

I imagine it will be of some consequence to you as a farmer to know that in all probability the Distillery will be suffer'd to work after Christmas, with an additional pretty high duty. Nothing is yet settled. The Committee meet on Thursday seven night. I think you may depend on the above intelligence.

Adieu

This appears to be a bit of inside information leaked from a Parliamentary committee affecting the brewery business in which Dell was closely involved at Aylesbury as well as in London. His sister Hannah married John Woodhouse – a London Wine Merchant and his sister Martha married John Delafield, another London merchant. An additional pretty high duty is being suggested by the committee and leaking this information was Wilkes' way of making amends for the refusal of the loan of his church pew three weeks earlier.

W/59 –Feb. 19 1760 Great George Street

Dear Dell

I agree with you as to the affair of the Overseers, that you are not to make a point of it, but I wish you to take the thorough pains to agree it with all parties and connections - if possible. I approve entirely your advice about the speaking to our friends at the Assizes, and the more for a reason, you cou'd not know.

Sir W H told me a few days ago, he was determined to push his friend at A and wou'd do all he could to serve me, and me in the first place. I bow'd but declared in the most express terms that I would stand on my own bottom, and would be entirely unconnected with the other candidates. I made no doubt of the affections of my own townsmen, and wou'd live on good terms with whoever else they chose without dictating to them who it should be. I will uniformly hold this language, and will always act up to it. Do you advise me to give a rout, and declare at once, with a supper to the independents, as soon as the Assizes are over? If you do, I will stay the Thursday in the Assize week, and do it. It may have disagreeable consequences, as to filling empty houses, making poor widows marry etc. I wish you to consider it, and give me your opinion in a post or two. Ch. L I fear wants the spirit necessary, tho' not the ammunition for the siege. Has Willes been at A or done anything since the races? I will bett he dies dunghill. The Ch Justice is dangerously ill. I have the most grateful letter in the world from Mr B and Mr H about their Commissions, with the strongest acknowledgements and professions. Do not the county people cry about, <u>two new uniforms to be sold very cheaply, little the worse for wear.</u> Miss Wilkes is perfectly well. The storm on Friday was the greatest I ever knew, and great damage has been done to the poor old, and new ill built houses here. I will confer with you about the barn etc. on Sunday 2nd March next, when I hope to dine at Aylesbury, and you with me. I beg my compliments to Mrs Dell and am ever, yours sincerely

John Wilkes

Things are beginning to hot up with talk of an impending election and prospective candidates are limbering-up. Sir W H* is talking of his friend joining Wilkes in the contest but Wilkes is determined not to become involved with others. He is still anxious to seek Dell's advice over yet another rout for the Independents to encourage continuing support. He is also questioning to whose advantage, from a voting point of view, it might be to marry-off any widows occupying houses; their new spouses would then qualify to vote as potwallers. (Is this another example of Wilkes' leg pulling or is he really serious with this weird suggestion?)

Charles Lowndes is also in the running but Wilkes has his doubts about him. John Willes' name has come up again; he was the other sitting member for Aylesbury at this time . Mr B and Mr H are clearly two who are in line for commissions in the Bucks Militia of which Wilkes was second in command.

W/60 – Nov. 4 1760 Great George Street

Dear Dell

After all the uproar and riots of that noisy Wilkes, I hear that you are all subsided into the calm and quiet of a country town, and I do not yet hear of any body who seems dispos'd to make chaos come again among you. Sure I am not alone to be the Atlas to support the sphere - The W...S have been to Lord I and Jack will come strongly into P's connection, felt his way for our Borough, but found no encouragement from Lord I who declar'd for me <u>alone</u> in terms which do me the highest honour. I believe they have quitted you entirely. Many overture to me, who still persisted and obstinately in the neutrality I have always declar'd for. This only to your private ear. Let Lord M..l...S's affair be still a secret. I have not mention'd it, but to you, whom I know I can trust - Lord I says, by no means – yet, no not near so soon as Christmas, but, let me beg you to take care of a house and remind Smith of the partition, sliding box etc. for we know not how soon a hurricane may succeed this dead calm, and as I am, like the women, always ready, so I wish Smith was. Pray tell him so with my best compliments. Nothing is yet settled, but everything to me wears the most smiling aspect - but whatever aspect it has, either out of the borough or in it, I shall ever etc. Dear Dell

affectionately yours John Wilkes

I have wrote letters of compliments to Bell, Price, Jack Smith, Minshull, Sir W.H., Sir W.Lee and Sir J Pack.

The death of King George in October of this year has made an election a certainty; at this time the death of the monarch was followed by an election. Edward Price was a solicitor and a Harding Trustee. The others mentioned in the letter were mostly those of influence with whom Wilkes had a passing acquaintance. Bell and Smith were locals but William Minshull was an attorney who became Clerk of the Peace for Buckinghamshire. Sir J Pack was Packington, Lord of the manor of Aylesbury; the family, whilst holding the title, had ceased to be resident in the town for many years. The manor was sold in 1802 to the Marquis of Buckingham. Sir W. Lee was of Hartwell. Minshull was probably George Minshull of Whitchurch.

W ... S. This is probably the Willes brothers, Edward and John. The latter had been the sitting member with Thomas Potter until Wilkes took the seat over in 1757. Lord I is probably Simon Lutterell, Baron Irnham, whose son Colonel Henry Lawes Luttrell opposed Wilkes' attempts to be elected for Middlesex a few years later. Although Lutterell lost the election to Wilkes, he was declared the winner by the House of Commons. The two, father and son, hated each other and the father once challenged his son to a duel but the later declined because he said his father was not a gentleman. Lord Irnham is said to have much enjoyed Wilkes' company.

W/61 – Nov. 11. 1760 Great George Street

Dear Dell

I am greatly oblig'd, and really think myself highly honoured by the generous support I find at Aylesbury - Not withstanding the opinion of Lord I. I mean (if you approve) -striking the blow at St Thomas's or rather the day after, which is Monday 22nd December. All this on the supposition that nothing particular from another quarter comes, which will precipitate it. I am therefore glad to hear of I.S.'s expedition about the house in Walton, which I hope is near finish'd – Mr Stephens has very obligingly wrote to me every particular about N..W's canvass, which has been more absurb than I cou'd have imagin'd. I wish however Cole had not been with him, for Cole is lively and high spirited - I find he pass'd the day at Bell's; do you find out, if he mollify'd him? Do you advise me to come to Aylesbury for two or three days between this, and St Thomas's, supposing you are all quiet, or may I stay here till then? Miss Wilkes may come perhaps for a week at Christmas - Pray write me your opinion, and mention all particulars which occur - I am ever, dear Dell, your oblig'd and affectionate friend.
John Wilkes. My compliments to Mrs Dell, and all friends with you. Did W only canvas the free V? Adieu

Things are hotting-up in Aylesbury and Wilkes has heard from Dell's brother-in –law, the Revd Stephens, that N.W. (Ned [Edward] Willes) has been campaigning in town. Wilkes is enquiring which of the voters Willes canvassed during his visit. Were they those already committed or some which are still open to persuasion? At a later stage he decided not to stand but Wilkes is on his guard should others surface and offer themselves.

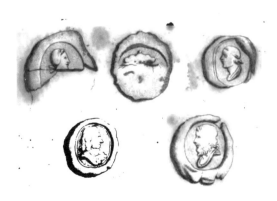

Seals used by Wilkes

Dear Dell

I think I can now promise you that the dead calm, which has so long lull'd you at Aylesbury, will be succeeded by a little blowing weather, tho' I hope not by a hurricane. I will tell you things in order of time. I have prevented a rich distiller from coming among you, mearly (sic) from fear of the jealousy his trade might give of a compromise with me. Wellbore Ellis being disappointed by Dodddington of coming in at his old place, has humbly petition'd his father in law Sir W.S. to recommend him to Aylesbury. Sir W catches at it, and will come down himself to canvas with the said wild boar - I have caution'd him much against taking Sir W with him, as the most fatal step he could take, and have reminded him of the famous declaration, "not a vote there, but I paid for" but it is all in vain, and next Monday or Tuesday, the red ribbon, and the solemn gravity of Ellis with you – I beg you loudly to trumpet forth my neutrality – Sir W makes Williams, Terry and Price, not one vote more himself – I forsee (sic) a certain opposition to Sir W's man, and of consequence double trouble and expense to myself. I will therefore be arm'd in compleat (sic) – not <u>steel</u> – but <u>gold</u>. Sir W has been with Ch.L received very coldly, and with a declaration that he did not yet know if he or his son stood – but, between ourselves, I know neither does - Ch.L talks of opposition to him in the county, and of putting up Sir Francis Dashwood. Dick Lowndes etc. proposed Aylesbury to Sir Francis, from what right I know not, but Sir Fr. is other wise engag'd. I certainly wish no opposition, but Sir W's canvas is a certain one, and I can neither stop that, nor the tide at London Bridge - If an opposition must come, rather let it be in this way, where I think the wild boar will share few of the independents with me - Perhaps management will do, but alas! I fear not with Hill etc. I have been much press'd, but will hold out no lights to Ellis. He will be embarrass'd for Agents etc. He swears that from the moment he embarks, he will spare no expense, and sacrifice his fortune to his own honour and Sir Wm's. - offer in everything to be directed by me - I will neither write nor speak on this head to any friend at Aylesbury - If Sir W did not at all interfere, perhaps Ellis wou'd do; but how to separate even in that case so near a relation from the idea of Sir W's friend and man, to be forced on a borough, which detests him - there I am embarrass'd, even in idea.- Perhaps after all I see Ellis's affair in too formidable a light - Pray write me your sentiments fully, and every particular that passes - Let me beg you to communicate to this letter immediately to Mr Stephens, and to Mr Smith; but desire it may remain a secret. I beg you to give me a line by Sunday night's post . Since I wrote the above, the D of N will, as far as he can, keep off all opposition, and therefore Ch. Lowndes must be quiet; but if an opposition <u>must</u> come, perhaps I had better send you a man after your own hearts - of spirit, honour and generosity. Adieu.

I have just rec'd a letter from a Dr Galpine of Wexham Green, near Slough in Bucks, who is coming to settle at Aylesbury as a Physician. He tells me he has a very good independent fortune and that I may depend on his vote. I wrote him a civil letter of acknowledgement.

I mean to come and make my bow in about 10 days.

Welbore Ellis (1713-1802), later 1ˢᵗ Baron Mendip, the member for Weymouth and Melcombe Regis, was forced to find another seat when George Bubb Doddington, Baron Melcombe, that town's patron, accepted another candidate at Prime Minister Bute's suggestion. Henry Fox, as Paymaster General, then proposed Aylesbury to him.

Ellis' father-in-law, Sir William Stanhope, who was an extensive landowner in Buckinghamshire, promised to come to Aylesbury in support of Ellis or The Wild Boar as Wilkes playfully calls him. Charles Lowndes who was involved with Wilkes in establishing of a branch of the London based Foundling Hospital opposed him and tried to interest Sir Francis Dashwood of West Wycombe in standing for the seat but in spite of Wilkes friendship with Sir Francis - both as members of the Hell Fire Club and of the Bucks Militia - he was "otherwise engaged". Indeed he was Member for New Romney and later Weymouth and Melcombe Regis under the patronage of Doddington. Dashwood was the Bucks Militia's first colonel with Wilkes its second in command.

Charles Lowndes' only son William was a governor of Christ's Hospital and the Westminster Infirmary. Williams and Price were fellow trustees of Hardings. The D of N was, of course, Thomas Pelham-Holles, 1ˢᵗ Duke of Newcastle, the supreme manager of the Whigs who was driven out of office the following year by Bute, King George's favourite. Wilkes at this stage was anxious for the duke to discourage others taking an interest in the Aylesbury seat.

W/63 – Friday Nov. 28 1760 Great George Street

Dear Dell

I wrote to you fully yesterday by the best conveyance, the post, about Mr Ellis's intention of coming to Aylesbury, and my idea of it. I hope you rec'd the letter. I have only to add that Mr Ellis sets out on Sunday, lies at Blackwells, and come to you early on Monday morning. Sir W sets out to morrow. Both are quite sanguine of success. Let me know if any thing is guess'd at by Sunday's post, and your full opinion. I have fifty great offers, but I keep to the firmness of my declaration. Lord M will certainly decline. He cannot get the ammunition for the siege. The advertisement for the Gentlemen etc. of Bucks, to nominate proper persons, to represent them in Parliament alarms the present Candidates very much - Dick L is thoroughly with me. If he writes to anybody, he will speak in the best terms of me, and of recommendation warmly; but he will not write at all, tho' Sir W has pressed him to the utmost for Ellis. Charles will not let Dick write a line for Ellis, and only in that case I have said I would be first nam'd and Dick has heartily agreed to it - I will come to Aylesbury, whenever you wou'd have me. Adieu.

Welbore Ellis and his father-in-law Sir William Stanhope have entered the fray and are preparing to come to Aylesbury. Wilkes is still considering his position but when he boasts that he has had "fifty great offers" i.e. to stand elsewhere, this was wishful thinking, or was he talking of promised votes? Ellis was said to have paid £5 for each voter in an electorate of around 500. His re-election in 1762 and 1765 respectively the figure was given as £3 to each voter. Dick L (Richard Lowndes) is willing to support Wilkes but it seems he will not commit himself in writing to the cause.

W/64 – Dec. 2 1760 Great George St.

Dear Dell

I have seen Sir William and Mr Ellis, who are return'd in high spirits and boast much of their reception. They talk at present of 5 – that is - you know 5 more candidates – nothing is determin'd, and that without danger is enormous - I shall come as soon as you are a little quiet, and talk it over with you – 42 I hear at supper – Bell, Price etc. I am impatient of your letter to-morrow – Bell wrote to me by Sir William and says the new candidate had great success – Willes wrote to Sir W.L. and desired his interest, was refused – this was only last Sunday. Goodnight

Sir William Stanhope and his son-in-law's are boasting of their visit to Aylesbury (W63) and of their favourable reception there which, of course, is worrying to Wilkes. Although mention of 5 is said to mean five more candidates, in effect it means £5 a head which if Wilkes is forced to match, may prove excessive. Brides are never spoken of openly in the letters but always referred to in hidden phrases.

The letter of which Wilkes speaks from John Willes to Sir W(illiam) L(ee) and his reply, is in the Lee Papers (D/LE/D11/58). Lee, in his reply said, "most of the people have told me they previously engaged to Mr Wilkes… I can influence very few beyond one vote."

W/65 – Dec. 23 1760 Great George Street

Dear Dell

I wrote last night, by the coach, and sent you the two books. I wish you to let me have as soon as you can a list of those you think worthy objects. They will not I hope much exceed 300. I think they need not. Pray particularly distinguish who among my company of militia shou'd have furloughs on the occasion, that I may write to Mr Gardiner about it. No time shall be lost. Is Liptrap's house ready? Pray engage every independent you can to dine at the White Hart with me on the election day - 4 certain,. 10 if necessary.

Yours most affectionate John Wilkes

The battle is on. The names of those thought by Dell worthy of Wilkes' opened purse are being sought. He is hopeful that 300 will be enough and the "fee at entry" is being talked-up as high as £10 but as the next implies he is hopeful that five guineas will do the trick.

W/66 – Dec. 27. 1760 Great George Street

Old Steady

I long for the account – what say you to 300 trees at 5 guineas a tree. Will that do? Then I have only good trees, but must I take every vile pollard, all the crazy wood too, of the whole forest – I shall very soon determine - The other perhaps not quite so soon. How operate the transactions of Monday. Adieu

In this letter four days after W/65, Wilkes is hopeful that five guineas will be enough but again in a hidden phrase he wants only those certain of supporting him to be included, questioning why he should take "every vile pollard and the crazy wood of the whole forest." In other words has he to pay out to those who are uncertain to support him.

W/18 – Tuesday December 30 (1760?) Great George Street

Dear Dell

I do not at all understand what this general councel (sic) to be held tomorrow means – I suspect no good to the present candidates – I beg as soon as you can to let me know what passes – Perhaps no body assists at it, or merely curiosity draws them all to it - I shall very soon bring down my great cannon, for I will carry the town at all events - Yet should they be charg'd with 4 or 5 pounders – I am clear at present with you for 4 and run the risks; but perhaps what passes tomorrow may alter your opinion – C.L. has not been in town till today; will write tonight. I have a dutiful letter from the Orator – I am thinking every day of coming to you. I empower you to make any declarations you judge necessary, and I will abide by them. I will have no petition, All my friends I will support to the utmost. It is as much for the honour of the borough as of myself to have your townsman put upon a different footing from a stranger – I come in my <u>post chaise</u> when? - talk of any time you like – the beginning of next week, when you will. Send Thorpe to town, if you think it proper. I received the books etc. Adieu.

Ever your affectionate friend   John Wilkes

Wilkes is querying with his friend how far he can go with handouts. The year of this letter is not given but by its content indicates that it is 1760. In October of that year King George died and this gave rise to an election the following year. Also the next.

Wilkes was fond of his nicknames. The Orator, also referred to in W/10 and W/13, would seem to have been a baker by the name of John Bass who probably was buried at Aston Clinton in 1765.

W/67 – Jan 1. 1761

Dear Dell

I am almost determin'd for to batter with five pounders. I think that is the clearest, most certain method of success. Can I set at defiance new voters and certificate men? Three hundred pick'd, and let the mongrels yelp their hearts out – I think in this case not quite so soon. When it is gone, there is with many no difference between never having had it, and the having it not – besides, their expectations still kept up, and less time to get others. Pray write as soon as you can, that I may determine. E has as yet no <u>thoughts of starting</u>. Adieu.

Wilkes seems confident that 300 five pounders will do the trick (i.e the number of promised votes at £5 a head) but asks if he can carry it off without the new voters and certificate men. See also W/63& W/66 in this content.

Having tested the water a month earlier when he and his father-in-law visited Aylesbury and was pleased with their reception, Ellis does not appear as yet to have started canvassing

W/68 – Jan 3 1761

Dear Sir

I beg you not to tear your beard off, as you threaten. Pray consider the soap manufacturer, and wou'd you have the Barbers starve? All trades must live. Consider you are a Maltster, besides Constable, Returning Officer etc. I am told this poll is to be taken in golden letters – to be serious. As I wrote last post, I think I am fixed for 5 pounders. You may if you please tell Smith or any body to declare it every where – then methinks I wou'd not give to a certificate man or voter made on purpose, that is if you approve. Select 300, bid the others to do their worst – I wou'd talk with Sir W and the wild boar – with 5, I am secure – shall I get them <u>to start first</u>, and to exclude the certificates and new ones, throw the odium on them, but follow the example – I must know certainly what they will do and cannot know that till next Wednesday – I rejoice that your Council ended as most general Councils have done. Give me a line <u>by the return of post.</u> Goodnight.

Wilkes is in a bantering mood. Something a frustrated Dell has written has amused him but pressure is building on the bribe front. By offering five(guineas), Wilkes feels sure of success but the certificate men and newcomers are to be excluded from the hand out. See the previous letter.

Sir W and the wild boar are Sir William Stanhope and his son-in-law Welbore Ellis who was one of Aylesbury's members between 1761-1768. See also W/64.

(The following letter is in the archives of the Bucks Archaeological Society. 516/39)

Jan 6. 1761 Great George Street.

All I have done is now nothing. I will never be Mr Bateman, but will equal any mad East or West Indian can be got - therefore pray declare strongly for five pounders. I do not think of less - but will not do anything yet - so I am advis'd by the wisest man I know here - I know something of electioneering and of Aylesbury. If W will batter with seven pounders, I will beat him, but will not yet; if he comes to-morrow - I see I am to fight it, as if my squinting phiz had never been seen at Aylesbury - so I will with the spirit I will do every thing but not yet. I am pronounced mad by my greatest and best friend here, if I do. Bass was here last night in good humour with me, mad with Ellis. I declared to him I should never offer less than 5 and if any body came, I would equal their highest performances. He will run the town for an opposition and swears he will be somebody's agent. He shall not be mine. I was very firm with him. I am more and more convinced that I am to wait, tho' my post-chaise and bureau have been long ready. Think how I am use'd: but I have steadiness and spirit, and I see my way thro' this and afterwards. Adieu, my dear Dell, and believe me ever

Your affectionate friend, John Wilkes

Pray write next post. Sir W talk'd of the first week in Jan. I chose Ellis should start first. I wish you find out how many are obliged to him.

Wilkes is clearly nervous. He thinks five pounders will carry the poll but nothing much less than this will do. He is even thinking of seven or more if Willes continues in the running but he is still unwilling to declare and a waiting game is still the preferred option in the hope that Ellis or Willes will lead the way. There is almost a tone of regret that, in spite of all he has done for the voters of the town, they are ungrateful and treat him as an outsider.

W/69 – Jan. 24 1761 Great George Street.

Dear Dell

I have the favour of your kind letter, and of Mr Stephens's. There are no two men I honour more. I am sure your advice is from the heart and your thorough opinion. I have agreed to the exorbitancy of 5, even against your and my other good friends' opinion. I honour you and the other gentlemen, who so generously support me: but I shou'd be unworthy of the protection you give me, if I was bulli'd by a mob. I have more than once declared, that they might receive all favours of every man who offers, and at last give their votes for their best friend, whom they will find me. I have reason both to despise the baseness of the vulgar, and their astonishing fickleness; but I am a philosopher and will sooner sell my estate among such wretches, and represent better men, worse I cannot, than be trampled upon. With this declaration, I will still come in a very short time, but I will never be ill-used, especially by those we both despise.
Adieu

His friends in Aylesbury have apparently advised him that five is the amount recommended which he considers exorbitant and he is smarting from the advice but accepting it. Never the less he still considers he is the voters' best friend even if they accept favours from every man who offers them. He is somewhat despairing of his fickle fellows but makes it clear that he would sell his estate and quit the town rather than be trampled upon by the vulgar mob.

W/70 – Jan. 27 1761 Great George Street.

Dear Dell

I wrote to you by the post on Saturday night, which I am surpris'd you have not receiv'd. I find the Parliament will not be dissolved as soon as was imagin'd. You wou'd avoid the present inconvenience and trouble, I provide for future safety. I told you by Saturday night's post that I lov'd and honour'd you, and a few more friends at Aylesbury, but that I would not be bulli'd by a mob. I know to the last, if any man offer a single shilling more, that I shall not be your member, but you know I will never be ill-us'd. A very few days hence I shall start, and I intend sometime the next week. By Thursday's post I shall write fully to you. I declare they shall have five guineas, or else I desire no vote, but I will never be trampled upon and I wou'd as here sell my estate at Aylesbury, and quit the Borough now as hereafter. I will bid up to the highest pitch of sanity anybody does for the Borough, and take my chance. I am to consider what I am to do, not only this, but in future times. If I am now master'd, adieu Borough. Pray enquire after the letter I wrote to you by the post on Saturday. Adieu

Wilkes is very close to entering the fray but in offering five (guineas) he has reached the limit of his resources and if a shilling more is offered he will call the whole thing off and "quit the borough".

W/5 – Sat. January 31 1761 Great George Street

Dear Dell

I thank you much for the favour of your letter. I can say little more to it, my heart is so full of grief, for my poor Father expired today, but without a pang or groan, only ceasing to breath. I wish that you and I, with every friend we have, may have as quiet and peaceful an exit. I am not at all alarmed with all the shameful reports which are propagated from Bierton against me. I thank Mr Hawkins most sincerely for his generous offers of money, which I have not the least occasion for, but the obligation of the tender I never will forget - The worthy objects of charity at Aylesbury I will certainly lend 5 guineas to, and the latest moment they shall have it, shall be on Tuesday seven nights, the 10th of February, perhaps the latter end of next week. The Parliament cannot rise two days before Easter holydays, as you may now be assur'd. If Mr W comes sooner than me, and lends 5 to the poor, I will lent 6, if he does 6, I will lend 7, if he 7, I 8 and so on I assure you. I desire you to let this be known to all my good friends at Aylesbury, whom I will support to the last, and who I am sure wou'd not have me be guilty of any disrespect to the ashes of a father, not only unburied, but scarcely cold, to whom I have such obligations. I know the nature of Aylesbury perfectly, and I feel at my heart the kindness of the Independents to me: but for the mercenaries, I am to buy them. If W gives any sum, the next day I will (for I know I can) go beyond it, and upon that, with the support of my disinterested friends I will carry Aylesbury. I beg you to show this letter, if not too foolish, to Mr Bell, Mr Stephens etc etc.and to write to me by the return of the post.

I am ever your affectionate and humble servant.   John Wilkes

In contrast to what he wrote a couple of days before when he threatened to quit rather than be bullied by a mob into paying a penny more (for the votes), the tone has changed and he will go higher to buy the mercenaries. Perhaps he is thinking that his father's death might help to ease his financial problems. In effect Israel left nothing in his will to add to his son's marriage settlement of 1741. The "shameful reports from Bierton" are probably coming from the Revd. Timothy Shaw, a thorn in Wilkes' flesh. See next W/71

W71 – February 5 1761   Great George Street

Dear Dell

I long to see the curiosities of Shaw's letters. He is the most ridiculous, bustling priest I have heard of - Pay F Carpenter the £20 bill, and thank him in my name for his civilities - I am not for lending to doubtful votes, nor certificate men - You mention Ellis'number as 322, out of which you say I shall refuse about 26, besides those who will not receive of one, but then some new ones will come in, so that I reckon about £1500 will do it.   I leave it to you but I fancy Liptrap shou'd talk of a second coming, because of absentees. I will write to you again on Saturday, as I suppose tomorrow's post will bring many queries and particulars from you or Smith. Adieu

Lipscomb in his History of Buckinghamshire describes the Revd. Timothy Shaw, vicar of Bierton, who kept a school in the village, as "indefatigable in the discharge of his ecclesiastical functions and one who ... frequently extended his assistance to the neighbouring clergy of less activity" and this ties in with Wilkes' description of him as "bustling". Consequently he was unlikely to have been very popular with his less energetic fellow priests in Aylesbury who were happy to carouse with Wilkes and his compatriots.

He is looking to challenge some of Ellis' voters and he himself is unwilling to "lend" (i.e. bribe) doubtful or certificate men. i.e. those outsiders who have been given Settlement Certificates on a temporary basis.

W/6 – undated but shortly after his father's death on 31 January 1761

Blackwells at Great Missenden

Dear Dell

Our good friend Mr Stephens will tell you the reason why I cou'd not possibly come here last night – I could not go out from Great George Street till yesterday morning from decency to my Father's memory, which prevents me from sending you as much cash as I intended. Mr Stephens' bag contains only 510 guineas. You would have had 500 more, had a friend of mine who has them kept his word as to his hour, but I could not wait. I have enclosed notes for £200, which you may use as you occasion. Be so good to send me an account of what notes are us'd by the return of post. I am ever gratefully and affectionately.

Yours John Wilkes

Pray declare Liptrap comes again to prevent discontents.

Wilkes, though in mourning for his father, is continuing to prepare for the forthcoming election. Funds are accumulating in Aylesbury in readiness of the proposed handouts. There is an indication, some time earlier, that Dell is nervous of having so much in his possession but Wilkes urges him to sleep soundly in his bed in spite of being responsible for the cash.

Clearly from this and other references (W/12 & W/63) Blackwells was an overnight stopping-off point for travellers of importance fairly near to Aylesbury. In effect Edward Blackwell was mine host at the White Hart in Great Missenden. In 1752, then aged 30, he was married at Little Missenden to Miss Mary Bigg (of Little Kimble). She seems to have been the daughter of John and Mary Bigg but any connection with other Biggs mentioned in the letters has not been established.

W/1 - Monday afternoon (sequence implied around this date in 1761)

Dear Dell

I send Samuel with 810 guineas. I shall follow with the rest, but I am afraid important business of the house will keep me till to-morrow morning: therefore do not begin at Aylesbury till tomorrow noon, if I am not come to Missenden, and adjourn till Wednesday morning. Nothing to be done by candlelight. I would not risk too much by one conveyance. What Samuel has in all events will last tomorrow's operation, and begin late; or if you chuse (sic) it, stay till Wednesday to finish.

Ever yours John Wilkes

Wilkes' messenger was probably his valet, Samuel Dryer.

W/7 – Saturday February 28 1761 Princes Court

Dear Sir

Mr Aubrey and I had the honour yesterday of presenting to the King at the levee the Aylesbury Address, and were received very graciously. I enclose you the account of the proceedings there faithfully printed from the copy, which you gave me. The Address will, I believe, be printed in the London Gazette on this night, but scarcely time enough to send you before Tuesday's post. The Public Advertiser therefore I thought could sooner gratify the public curiosity and consequently the address too appears there. I am happy to find it meets with a most generous approbation and for the composition it has been applauded even by the present opposition. I desire you to assure my good friends at Aylesbury that I shall always receive their commands with deference, and obey them with alacrity. The obligations which they formerly conferred on me, are still fresh in my memory.

I am always Dear Sir

Your affectionate humble servant   John Wilkes

Miss Wilkes desires her compliments

The Aylesbury Address presented at the levee by Wilkes and Aubrey was probably one made by the loyal townsfolk of the town upon the accession of George the Third. In 1769, as Aylesbury's newly elected member, John Aubrey of Chilton and Boarstall championed Wilkes' cause in his battle with the government.

W/8 – Tuesday March 17 (1761) Great George St.

Dear Sir

Everything continues for the writs issuing on Saturday morning so that you may proclaim the election for the Wednesday following. I shall go towards Marlow on Thursday. I mean to be on Thursday night at the Castle at Salt Hill, and so on to Marlow on Friday morning. I shall then grant furlongs for ten days to every Aylesbury man in my Company – Pray send somebody over to Medmenham as soon as ever you receive the Writt. I shall not go from hence till (sic) the Tuesday so as to be at Aylesbury that afternoon, unless you want me sooner. Do not mention anything as to my not intending to come till the Tuesday, but tell everybody you do not know where I am but that you expect me everyday after Saturday – this will prevent all idle application from any of our people.

Adieu Dear Dell and believe me ever your sincerely

John Wilkes

Wilkes had become active in the Bucks Militia commanded by Sir Francis Dashwood at West Wycombe. Its resurgence was part of Pitt's overall war strategy for this voluntary home defence force and released soldiers to serve overseas. Clearly Wilkes was with his regiment close to Marlow and was about to grant ten day's furlough to his men from Aylesbury to enable them to vote in the election that was being planned. But until the writ reached Dell as Returning Officer, nothing was to be made public "to prevent all idle application from any of our people". It was also intended to keep the information of the forthcoming election a secret and prevent others contemplating becoming candidates. The fewer putting-up meant less to bribe.

W/72 – April 21 1761 Great George St.

Dear Dell

I have well weig'd everything respecting my affairs at Aylesbury, both as member, and as a private gentleman having an estate in the borough. After so many and so various acts of kindness to many individuals, I found what I had to trust from the majority. I never thought my interests at A of any consequence; I have found it not of the least. I was work'd up to the high-watermark of Ellis, and shall be of Delaval or Clive if I expect to carry the borough again, and either of them attempt it. When I have said this, I add too that I know myself and love to do acts of humanity and feel a real sense of gratitude towards the few independents, who have oblig'd me. I wish to give them pleasure at A, here, everywhere: but I will not be the dupe of the mob, nor a few wretched impertinents. I was tir'd, when I was last in the country, with the stories I was told, some of which I found true, of the insolence of some of the inn-keepers etc. and the imposing spirit of more. I talked to Stephens and Thorpe about their proceeding in a few instances, and have given Thorpe orders by the post tonight to keep away from the house and gardens, all the rabble at A. If any of the better sort choose at any time to walk in the gardens, the gardener shall attend them, as is done everywhere else, and then I shall get rid of the numbers of women, children, dogs, etc. You would stare at the number of little thefts they make. I mean the lower sort: the best flowers etc. etc. I shall be glad, whenever the gardens can afford pleasure to the better sort at A, and would at times accommodate them with anything out of them. I have directed Thorpe to keep the gates always bolted and whoever rings, he will attend, and will go with any company round the garden. As to your private door, I object greatly on account of the servants, and therefore will scruple no expense to make the well answer the purpose of a well. I have seen ill blood arising. I can scarcely manage my own servants, much less yours too: and the only way for the preservation of any harmony, is to keep them distinct. When the well is done, your servants can have no business with mine in the Parsonage yard; mine none with yours, except the trifles of dung etc. when I am down which is but seldom and likely to be seldomer. . I follow Stephen's advice of sending twice a week to town, the proceeds of the kitchen garden and pigeons etc. and intend the same hamper shall often bring me fowls and butter etc. for which I pay exorbitantly here. I give Stephens a key and desire whenever you or Mrs Dell chose to walk in the garden you wou'd, without Thorpe and with the children at any time: but do not send servants with them. Do not suspect me of peevishness. I am much above it, and desire equal, and constant good humour as one of the first blessing of heaven – but I see farther than you into this, and therefore stop it in time.

Miss Wilkes desires her compliments. I was wet thro' in a hour today, and am not the worse – hope the country is the better and wish it had all the rain I have had. I am ever,

Dear Dell

Your affectionate friend   John Wilkes

I wish the kitchen finish'd as soon as can be.

Although he has only just been re-elected in the poll that followed the death of King George the Second, Wilkes is in a thoroughly bad mood when he considers what the votes have cost him. Secure for seven years, the then span of elected Parliament, he is able to let fly at the wretched impertinents who, as he sees it, take advantage of his good will in petty ways; picking the best flowers in his much admired garden and so on. He is even anxious to prevent his servants fraternising with those of Dell at the communal well in the Parsonage Yard. Being soaked to the skin earlier in the day has not improved his temper although he is anxious not to sound peevish to his good friend – old steady - and is happy for him and his family to walk in the garden.

W/73 – September 12 1761   Great George Street

Dear Dell

Your ticket and apartment are ready, and I hope in civility you will come some time before to see Miss Wilkes and me, not merely for the show. I never saw anything like the greatness of the preparations going on. I kissed the Queen's fair hand on Thursday. I hope my gamekeeper does not forget me as scarcely feather or lever have yet reached me - I have a most fawning letter from Shaw, for which I despise him, if possible, more than ever. I have return'd a true Courtier's answer.

I am ever Dear Dell

Your sincere friend   John Wilkes

This was the occasion of the coronation of King George the Third. Dell and his wife were the guests of Wilkes, not in the Abbey, but in a stand seat outside. Timothy Shaw, the vicar of Bierton, is also mentioned in W/71. Perhaps here he had been angling for an invitation to the Coronation.

Wilkes is back to his favourite domestic subject of game. What is Lever? Could it be a leveret – a young hare being considered game.

W/74 – January 1. 1762

(To Sergeant Green)

Great George Street

I shall be at Aylesbury the 9th of this month, and intend to stay the week. What you want till then for yourself and the other Sergeants and Drummers of my Company, call on Mr Dell Jnr and he will advance the money to you. Shew him this letter. I leave everything of my company to be settled when I come to Aylesbury; and order the Sergeant Major from me, my two other Sergeants, and the two drummers with the fife, to come there by the 12th.

Yours John Wilkes

Is this one of Wilkes coded letters or is he really talking about the Militia in which he served as an officer? He was dismissed the following year when he was committed to the Tower of London. Could it be a reference to Dell himself and his fellow supporters in Aylesbury? Dell's wife was a Miss Green before her marriage in 1752. (Her family was descended from William of Wykeham, founder of New College Oxford). In addressing this letter to "Sergeant Green" could this be an example of Wilkes' perverted sense of humour and continuing need for secrecy that dominates the correspondence. To whom is he referring when he speaks of Mr Dell Junior. There is no Dell Senior apart from Dell himself and his own son is only six. This is probably aimed at his close supporters in Aylesbury formerly under his command in the militia, his other Sergeants and two drummers with the fife and Dell himself, the Sergeant Major. Whether Dell in real life was a member of the Bucks Militia under Wilkes, is not known.

W/75 – February 26 1763 Great George St.

Dear Dell

I had the favour of yr letter and was very sorry to hear the season had been so sickly at Aylesbury. The accounts from Cambridgeshire are still more unfavourable. I had sent Sergeant Green a £10 note before I had your letter – I suppose he has repaid you the two guineas as he has not charged them in his account.
You may at any time advance him five guineas , but not more and let him repay you, as soon as what I send him comes if by accident I miss a few days, which I believe I shall not.
Miss Wilkes is, I thank heaven, perfectly well and much delighted with the future idea of Paris. My compliments attend Mrs Dell, Dr & Mrs Stevens etc.

I am ever Dear Dell
Yours sincere friend and humble servant JW

L.Sh. told me he had seen some Aylesbury voters who damned H for a coward.

Read in conjunction with W/74, most of this letter is hard to interpret. The finance discussed clearly relates to handouts. Is Sergeant Green really John Dell?

L.Sh is probably Lord Shelburne and H is William Hogarth, the satirical painter and engraver who in 1763, the year of this letter, drew what has become the best-known caricature of John Wilkes.

William Petty Lansdowne (1737-1805), by this date Lord Shelburne, was president of the Board of Trade and a prominent politician of the day. Wilkes was trying to obtain a governmental position but without success. Shelburne was well known to Wilkes but the latter's reaction to the unflattering portrayal is not recorded.

W/17 – Sat. Nov. 29 (1766) Princes Court

Mr Wilkes presents his compliments to Mr Dell and desires to return many thanks for a present of very delicate pig-meat. He had a letter yesterday from Miss Wilkes, who is in perfect health at Paris on a visit to the Duchess de la Valliere.

W/76 - July 9 1768 King's Bench Prison

I have been so much engaged in the variety of business which I have had for several weeks that it has not been in my power before to thank you for your very obliging letter. I am truly sensible of the kind parts my friends at Aylesbury take in whatever concerns me, and I beg you to accept yourself, and make them, my best acknowledgement.

The old bottled beer you were so kind as to send me is much liked and I have a particular pleasure in drinking your health and the County Town of Bucks in its produce.

I desire my best respects to your family and to your two excellent parsons, Dr Stephen & Mr Pugh, whom I always think of with the greatest pleasure. Miss Wilkes sends her compliments to you and Mrs Dell.

Gillam, the Justice, who gave the order for the firing at the late massacre here, is to be tried this afternoon.

I am ever, Dear Sir, your affectionate & humble servant

A few years have passed since the last letter. Wilkes, after his conviction, is languishing in the King's Bench Prison and is clearly catching-up on his correspondence.

An effort was made to prosecute Magistrate Samuel Gillam for ordering soldiers to shoot innocent bystanders on 10 May 1768 during the riots in St George's Fields. The Middlesex Grand Jury found him guilty of the crime on 7th July but the verdict was reversed at the Old Bailey a few days later.

W/77 – Nov. 10 1768 King's Bench Prison

Mr Wilkes present his compliments to Mr Dell and has only time to return many thanks for the obliging letter of the 6th and to assure him and all his family of the regard Mr W ever bears them.

W/9 – Mon afternoon March 29 (1773) Princes Court

My dear Dell

I have but a moment to thank you for your very friendly letter, and to say that I am sure you will do right, and I wish every election at Aylesbury may likewise. I do not know of any opposition to me for Middlesex. Many thanks for your good wishes. I enclose you my address. I desire to be affectionately remember'd to all our friends. Adieu

Wilkes connection with Aylesbury is drawing to a close after his return from outlawry, subsequent battles with Parliament over his wrongful arrest and his continuing expulsions from the house in spite of being re-elected twice for Middlesex. He is aiming for higher things that culminated in his election as Lord Mayor of London in 1774.

W/16 Saturday October 2 (1773) Princes Court Westminster

My dear Friend

I imagined the transactions of Monday relative to the nomination of a county Member will be very interesting. I wished to have been present, but as the vacancy in my own county will detain me here, I shall esteem it a particular favour, if you will take the trouble of giving me the account of it by Tuesday's post. I wish to know how the pulse of the county beats, and what party your neighbour Lord Chesterfield takes. I beg my services to your family in particular, and all our friends at Aylesbury and believe me.

Dear Dell, your affectionate friend & humble servant, John Wilkes

I shall be obliged to you for all the handbills circulated on the occasion.

This is nearing the end of the correspondence between the two men. Wilkes is busy with his national campaign that culminated in his election the following year as Lord Mayor of London. His connection with Aylesbury is now only marginal but he is still showing an interest in its parliamentary affairs. The county member to which Wilkes refers was probably John Aubrey described as a "rich country gentleman". He defeated Anthony Bacon, a merchant and arms contractor, who had stood for Aylesbury upon Wilkes expulsion from the House in 1764. Lord Chesterfield's influence in the borough is still of interest to Wilkes. See W/7 and W/78 on Aubrey.

My dear Sir

I have the favour of your letter of the 20th and as I understand that Mr Aubrey's brother is at Bath, I will make immediate application to him, and probably he will be in time.

Miss Wilkes & I pass the holidays here. We came only for amusement, enjoying, thank heaven, both of us at present, perfect health.

I have not any connection with Lord Verney.

 I desire to be kindly remember'd to all your family and am ever Dear Dell

Yours affectionate friend and humble servant

John Wilkes

Sir John Aubrey (1739-1826) of Chilton and Boarstall did not enter into to the baronetcy until 1786 but is mentioned elsewhere in the letters. Which of his two brothers is referred to here is not known or is what Wilkes is to make "application" about.

This is the final letter in the series and there is no interpretation as to its content. Dell is addressed as "My dear Sir" and as one of Wilkes biographers has noted he was inclined to forget the services of his docile satellites as soon as they were no longer useful to him. Once Wilkes' Aylesbury properties were sold in 1764, the link with the borough and its inhabitants was broken forever. Sir William Lee of Hartwell appears to have purchased the bulk of the interest. The whole property, apart from the house and garden was sublet to John Dell at £250 per annum.

Wilkes Tomb in Grosvenor Chapel